THE

HURDY-GURDY

IN

EIGHTEENTH-CENTURY

FRANCE

Publications of the Early Music Institute

Thomas Binkley, general editor

THE
Hurdy-Gurdy
IN
Eighteenth-Century France

ROBERT A. GREEN

Indiana
University
Press
BLOOMINGTON AND INDIANAPOLIS

The paper used in this publication meets the minimum requirements of the American National Standard for Information Sciences—Permanence of Paper for Printed Library Materials, ANSI Z39.48-1984.

Manufactured in the United States of America

Library of Congress Cataloging-in-Publication Data

Green, Robert A., date
      The hurdy-gurdy in eighteenth-century France/ Robert A. Green.
        p.   cm. — (Publications of the Early Music Institute)
      Includes bibliographical references (p.   ).
      ISBN 0-253-20942-0 (alk. paper)
      1. Hurdy-gurdy. 2. Music—France—18th century—History and criticism. I. Title. II. Series.
      ML1086.G73 1995
      787.6'9'094409033—dc20   94-29618

1 2 3 4 5 00 99 98 97 96 95   MN

CONTENTS

ILLUSTRATIONS

PREFACE

The hurdy-gurdy has been in continuous use in Western Europe for a thousand years: few other instruments can make that claim. In the thirteenth and eighteenth centuries it was found in the most musically cultivated circles: in the fourteenth through the seventeenth centuries, it was played by the lowest classes. Today, it is a popular folk instrument in France, much like, for example, the banjo in American music.

The story of the hurdy-gurdy, or, as it is known in France, the vielle, is so interesting that much has been written about its use in different periods. In such surveys, the cultivation of the vielle in eighteenth-century France represents only a chapter, but so many beautiful instruments and so much information, relatively speaking, survives from this period that it has received more attention than any other. Nevertheless, there are many areas left to explore, and surprisingly, the music composed for the vielle and its performance is one of these.

Previous explorations of the vielle during the eighteenth century have revealed a certain blindness on the part of most authors. They have focused on its cultivation by lady amateurs at the highest level of society, most notably members of the French royal family, leaving the impression that fashion rather than musical considerations was largely responsible for the popularity of the instrument. In addition, most authors have not been players of the instrument and have failed to grasp the distinctive features of the repertory. I believe that these two considerations are largely responsible for a lack of interest in the vielle among those concerned with eighteenth-century music and its performance on period instruments. Thus the purpose of this book is to place the instrument squarely within of the purview of the latter group.

This book is written with two types of audience in mind: those interested in eighteenth-century music and what the vielle and its music can reveal about the sound world of the period, and those who play the instrument and are familiar with the fundamentals of technique but wish to explore the interpretive possibilities. This book is not a method. Elements of technique are discussed only insofar as they are necessary for the general reader to understand musical and performance practice considerations.

In order to fully understand what is said here, it is important that the reader understand my biases. I became aware of the vielle and its music through my musicological research into the instrumental music of the early eighteenth century. I found so many interesting works that I wanted to play them and find out how they sounded on the instrument for which they were written. Eventually I was able to acquire a good instrument and learned to play it by reading the eighteenth-century methods discussed in detail here. There was much left unexplained, however, and I went to France to learn more about the technique from the players of folk music who have studied the instrument as part of a living tradition. I soon encountered several who were interested in the eighteenth-century repertory, but who approached their examination of this literature and study of the treatises from their background as folk musicians. While many of these players have a thorough grounding in technique based on their involvement with folk music, it is difficult for them to discard elements of their playing which they have found to be expressive but which are inappropriate, or used in a different way, in the performance of the eighteenth-century literature. I differ from them in that I have approached this music from my background as a scholar and one who is generally familiar with what was composed for other instruments in the period. Thus the issue in learning to play and interpret the music then becomes what to retain from the living tradition as musically valid and what to discard as inappropriate. No player fully agrees here, and, therefore, widely differing approaches may be heard in performances of this music. The same must be said of any other instrument, however, but with more and more performances of the music for the vielle, a range of musically viable possibilities will emerge.

I must mention here Claude Tailhades, who served first as a mentor in my learning to play the instrument and then as a collaborator in an exploration of the duo literature, a literature we had hoped to record. Claude, one of the finest players in France, turned his attention from folk music to the eighteenth century about ten years ago. Of all the players in France he, in my opinion, most successfully combined his knowledge of the technique derived from the living tradition with what he learned from the treatises. Although we differed on minor points, our views on the major ones were alike. Much of what is said in Chapter Three resulted from our continuing dialogue on issues of performance practice. Although Claude's death on January 12, 1995 brought an end to our collaboration, I can only hope that this book will serve in some way as a memorial to his contribution.

If my attitudes have been influenced by my experiences as a player, they have also been influenced by the instruments themselves. The outstanding reproductions of eighteenth-century vielles by Thomas Norwood of Paris and an eighteenth-century instrument from about 1740 built by François Feury and restored by Norwood have strongly influenced the formation of a sound ideal. The hurdy-gurdy is a complex mechanism which requires considerable adjustment. These adjustments can change the sound considerably, and, therefore, one must know what sound one wants. The paradox is that one does not know what sound one wants until one has heard it. It was only after considerable experimentation that I arrived at the sound I wanted and which best served the music, and I have tried to communicate this ideal as well as words can describe it. When I first began to play the instrument, I thought of it as a diversion. The sound was so intensely satisfying, however, that I could not put the instrument down. Over the years I have encountered many players of various abilities all united by their love of the sound of the instrument. It is therefore difficult for me to believe that eighteenth-century players did not on some level share that attraction whether or not the instrument was fashionable. After giving lecture recitals and concerts at universities and as part of various early music series, I made a recording *French Music for Hurdy-Gurdy* (FOCUS 932) which realizes many of the ideas on interpretation presented in this book. In addition it recreates the sound world of eighteenth-century France as it relates to the vielle by including a spectrum of music from the unaccompanied arrangement of music for other instruments to chamber music in the latest style.

In introducing the reader to the eighteenth-century literature for the hurdy-gurdy, I have not hesitated to express my critical judgment regarding the relative merits of various works in order to separate the interesting from the mundane. Although value judgments of this kind must include an element of subjectivity based on the satisfaction derived from playing the music, two questions truly provided the basis for these remarks: Does this music use the instrument to its full capabilities? Does the composer create harmonic variety within the limitations imposed by the drones? Rhythmic variety and contrapuntal interest were also taken into account.

Finally, this book is not the last word on the vielle and its music in eighteenth-century France. A thorough study of the popular airs and dances played as pastime music by the large majority of eighteenth-century players, now being undertaken by Françoise Bois-Poteur, will add significantly to our knowledge of the literature. No complete catalogue of instruments surviving from the eighteenth century with their measurements and descriptions now exists, and until such a project is completed, it will be difficult to discuss the contributions of various makers and their distinctive characteristics. A thorough search of the memoirs of various members of the court and society in the early eighteenth century, as well as legal documents housed in national and regional archives, may reveal more about the composers and teachers, the amateurs who played the instrument, and the few virtuosi who made a career performing on the instrument.

No project of this kind is undertaken in a vacuum. I want to thank Northern Illinois University for providing me with summer grants and a sabbatical to complete this book. My thanks to Rick Hirsch for his speedy and accurate preparation of the musical examples and to Peter Middleton for the loan of his equipment for the preparation of camera-ready copy. Thanks also to Dr. Warren R. Jones of Loyola University of Chicago for a careful, thoughtful reading of the manuscript. I also want to express my appreciation to the editor Nathalie Wrubel for her many suggestions and her support and encouragement. I want to express my special gratitude to Lee Chapman, who as an intelligent listener provided a sounding board for many ideas and read successive drafts providing much useful and constructive criticism. This effort is immeasurably the better for his advice.

CHAPTER ONE

HISTORICAL BACKGROUND

Terminology

The English term hurdy-gurdy is used to describe two different instruments. First, there is the mechanical organ with a mechanism much akin to that of a player piano which was played earlier in this century by immigrants who begged for money with monkeys and tin cups on the street corners of American cities. These instruments are still found in European parks and on street corners and are differentiated from the hurdy-gurdy by other names, such as *orgue de Barbarie* in French. For many, the term hurdy-gurdy first calls to mind this instrument. Much less familiar is the instrument whose sound is produced by a rosin-coated wheel which, like a bow, rubs against several strings. This wheel is turned by a crank. Some of these strings function as melody strings, others as drones, giving the instrument a sound like that of a bagpipe.

This latter instrument is found throughout continental Europe as far east as western Russia and may be the only instrument truly indigenous to that continent. It has a history which goes back to the eleventh century. In different times and in different regions, it has taken many shapes and been given different names. All European languages, however, with the exception of English, differentiate between the mechanical organ and the bowed instrument. No other language or group of people draw parallels between these two instruments.

The following discussion centers around the bowed instrument as it appeared and was used in eighteenth-century France. It is therefore appropriate to refer to it by the name by which it was known in that time in that place: the vielle.

Social Life in the Seventeenth Century

No musical instrument has suffered so grievously from changes in social status. In eleventh-century Germany, the vielle was associated with church music.[1] By the twelfth century it was associated with music performed in the courts of the nobility. By the fourteenth century it had become associated with lower classes and eventually, by the fifteenth century, it became associated with blind beggars. Blindness was regarded as a physical manifestation of inner or moral blindness, and, therefore, the very appearance of the instrument in a painting suggested sin.[2] Although certain painters at the beginning of the seventeenth century, such as Rembrandt van Rijn (1606-1669) and Georges de la Tour (1593-1652), began to regard blind vielle players as victims of a tragic infirmity, the instrument retained its repellent reputation.

The views toward blind beggars and their instruments are reflected in the introduction to Mersenne's oft-quoted description of the vielle in *Harmonie universelle* of 1636.

> If men of rank played the vielle as a rule, it would not be regarded with such contempt. But because it is played only by the poor, and particularly by blind men who earn their living from this instrument, it is held in less esteem than others, but then it is not as pleasing. This does not stand in the way of what I will explain here, since science belongs to both rich and poor, and there is nothing so low and vile in nature that it not be worthy of discussion.[3]

---

[1]For a thorough investigation of the medieval instrument, see Christian Rault, *L'Organistrum* (Paris: Aux Amateurs de Livres, 1985). See also Christopher Page, "The Medieval *Organistrum*: A Legacy from the East?," *The Galpin Society Journal* 35 (1982): 37-44, and "The Medieval *Organistrum* and *Symphonia*: 2 Terminology," *The Galpin Society Journal* 36 (1983): 71-87. These two authors do not agree on several features of this subject.

[2]On the representation of the hurdy-gurdy in art from the late fifteenth century to the beginning of the seventeenth century, see Kahren Jones Hellerstedt, "Hurdy-gurdies from Hieronymus Bosch to Rembrandt," diss., U of Pittsburgh, 1981. Dr. Hellerstedt includes a list of 168 representations.

[3]Marin Mersenne, *Harmonie universelle contenant la théorie et la pratique de la musique* (Paris, 1636), Traité des instrumens à chordes, 211-212: "Si les hommes de condition touchoient ordinairement la Symphonie, que l'on nomme *Vielle*, elle ne seroit pas si mesprisée, mais parce qu'elle n'est touchée que par les pauures, & particulierement par les aueugles qui gaignent leur vie auec cet instrument, l'on en fait moins d'estime que des autres, quoy qu'ils ne donnent pas tant de plaisir. Ce qui n'empesche pas que ie ne l'explique icy, puis que la science n'appartient pas dauantage aux riches qu'aux pauures, & qu'il n'y a rien de si bas ny de si vil dans la nature, ou dans les arts qui ne soit digne de consideration."

Mersenne goes on to point out that if someone took an interest in the instrument and

Social attitudes towards the instrument in the early part of the seventeenth century based on Mersenne and other writers have been discussed in detail.[4] A number of civil documents surviving from the seventeenth century and published in secondary sources indicate that however poor players of the vielle in the first part of the seventeenth century may have been, they often had families, a place to live, and legalized the events of their lives, such as births, deaths and marriages, as did every other citizen.[5] Documents indicate that at least some players took musician-apprentices, as did other musicians of the period. Some were members of the *Corporation St. Julien-des ménétriers* so viciously satirized by François Couperin (1668-1733) in his piece *Les fastes de la grande et anciénne Mxnxstrxndxsx* from Book II (1716-1717). The "Seconde Acte" of this piece entitled "Les Viéleux et les Gueux" ("the vielle players and beggars") consists of two "airs de viéle." The piece accurately reflects the sound of the vielle with its c-g drones; however, the satirical element must be taken with a grain of salt. The music limps along, evoking the decrepit condition of those who played the instrument. Couperin devoted much of his efforts to gaining a noble title, and his desire to separate

---

refined it, that it would be capable of playing music which would "touch the spirit" as much or more so than other instruments. Even so, he feels that the nature of the instrument is such that its possiblities are limited. He discusses a hypothetical keyboard instrument which would produce its sound with either a series of rosined wheels or one big wheel like the vielle. To Mersenne, it would sound like a consort of viols.

[4]For example, Richard Leppert, *Arcadia at Versailles* (Amsterdam and Lisse: Swets & Zeitlinger B.V., 1978): 11-32.
See also Frayda B. Lindeman, "Pastoral Instruments in French Baroque Music: Musette and Vielle," diss. Columbia U., 1978, 81-86.

[5]There are two major sources of biographical information for seventeenth-century Parisian musicians not associated with the court. The "Laborde affiches," a file containing 66,080 entries from parish records and other sources referring to musicians in the sixteenth, seventeenth, and eighteenth centuries, contains the names of nine "joueurs de vielle" between 1620 and 1646. The entries associated with these musicians give addresses and mention baptisms and marriages. Only one of these is explicitly described as "pauvre aveugle" (poor blind man). The second source consists of legal documents in the National Archives in Paris. For the first, see *Musiciens de Paris 1535-1792. Actes d'état civil d'après le fichier Laborde de la Bibliothèque Nationale.* Ed. Yolande de Brossard. Vie musicale en France sous les rois Bourbons 11 (Paris: A. et J. Picard & Cie, 1965). For the second, see Madeleine Jurgens, *Documents du Minutier Central concernant l'histoire de la musique (1600-1650)* (Paris: S. E. V. P. E. N., 1967), which lists an additional player in an entry dated 1605. Claude Tailhades, "Viellistes de ville - Viellistes de Cour" (unp. essay), 1993, searched these two works and listed the names of these players.

himself from the lowly status associated with the professional musician must be borne in mind.

The first documented appearance of the vielle at the French court is its use in the *Ballet de l'impatience* presented at the Louvre on February 19, 1661. The Third Entrée of Part IV (LWV 14/47-50) begins with an instrumental introduction for the entrance of blind beggars. This is followed by an instrumental section labelled "ten blind men impatient of losing time for earning a living." A récit follows which in mock solemnity compares the unfortunate situation of the blind men with love that can be as blind as they are. The blind men then play an air on the vielle. The music contrasts with what proceeds and follows in its diatonic and harmonically static nature: it is clearly composed with drones in mind. This piece would have been performed with the vielles on the top line doubled and accompanied by the five-part string ensemble (see Example 1).

Example 1.   Jean-Baptiste Lully, *Ballet de l'impatience* (LWV 14/50). "Second air pour les aveugles jouant de la vielle." In this example the middle parts have been removed.

The vielle was further used in Lully's *Ballet des sept planètes*, composed of ten entrées which concluded the performance of *Hercule amoureux* (*Ercole amante*) by Francesco Cavalli on February 7, 1662. The pilgrims are given a piece for vielles and ensemble (LWV 17/21). This ballet following so closely on the *Ballet de l'impatience* suggests that the instrument was regarded as a novelty, but using it twice seems to have been enough for Lully: He never composed music for it again.

Due to the paucity of sources dealing with the vielle in seventeenth-century France and its increasing use among the aristocracy, most writers have come to depend on the history of the vielle published by Antoine de Terrasson (1705-1782) in 1741.[6] Terrasson republished his account in 1768 revealing his lifelong enthusiasm for the instrument.[7] Terrasson was a musical amateur who played the musette, flute and vielle, as well as a jurist and man of letters who was well equipped to argue a case. His purpose is to demonstrate that the vielle deserves respectability due to its antiquity. Tracing the origins of the instrument he links it with ancient Greece and the lyre of Orpheus. While it is all too easy to attack the obvious inaccuracies in his discussion of Greek myths and music history, as many writers have done, it is well to remember that many instrumental treatises use exactly the same arguments to demonstrate the great age and therefore respectability in making a case for the importance of other instruments.[8] Nevertheless when Terrasson arrives at the period within the living memory of the people around him, he demonstrates profound understanding of the evolution of his instrument. Terrasson describes the arrival, perhaps the result of an invitation from an enthusiastic courtier, of two vielle players named "La Roze" and "Janot" at court some time after the first operas of Lully, which stimulated an interest in the instrument

---

[6]Antoine de Terrasson, *Dissertation historique sur la vielle* (Paris: J.B. Lamesle, 1741).

[7]Antoine de Terrasson, *Mélanges d'histoire, de littérature, de jurisprudence litteraire, de critique* (Paris, Chez la veuve Simon & fils, 1768): 173-254. Neal Zaslow, "Charles Bâton," *The New Groves Dictionary of Music and Musicians* (London: MacMillan Publishers Limited, 1980), suggests that Bâton was in fact the author of the *Dissertation*. The internal evidence overwhelmingly suggests otherwise. For example, in the forward to the *Mélanges*, Terrasson clearly introduces the *Dissertation* as his own. However, the technical detail contained in this work suggests that Terrasson received considerable advice from either Charles or Henri. Further, Terrasson's praise of Charles Bâton's sonatas in the 1768 long after the latter's death demonstrates the former's strong allegiance to the composer.

[8]For example, Borjon de Scellery, *Traité de la musette* (Lyon: Girin Riviere, 1672): 1-13, traces the origins of the musette back to antiquity.

among the aristocracy.[9] His discussion of the appearance of the vielle at
court after 1671, possibly about 1680, appears to be based on testimony
which can to some degree be corroborated from other sources.[10]

Throughout this period the vielle shared its existence with the musette,
a small bagpipe played by bellows pumped by the left elbow and
requiring no breath from the player.   This instrument had become
fashionable with the upper classes in the early seventeenth century and
continued to be popular until the end of the reign of Louis XV (about
1770) after which time, it became extinct as a result of changing taste.
This contrasts with the vielle which has been played continuously until
the present.   The musette was cultivated by families of professional
players attached to the court musical establishment: the Hotteterres and
the Chédevilles. It became an accepted orchestral instrument and has
frequent, and sometimes extensive, parts in the great French operas of the
early eighteenth century. Much of the music for the vielle is also playable
on the musette and vice versa.

The Eighteenth Century

What is often overlooked in Mersenne's discussion of the vielle in the
Harmonie universelle (1636) is his speculation on how the vielle could be
improved. This flexibility, the ability of makers to alter it to conform to
changing musical styles and social function, has characterized the
instrument since its origins, and would be the basis for its growth in
popularity throughout the eighteenth century.

It seems likely that the vielle began its rise in society in the late
seventeenth century with the development of a slightly more refined
instrument with a characteristic shape described by Terrasson as a "vielle

---

[9]Terrasson (1741): 89-93. Both played popular airs and dances including selections from
the operas of Lully. They sometimes sang while accompanying themselves on the vielle.

[10]Marcelle Benoit, *Versailles et les musiciens du roi*. La vie musicale en France sous les
rois Bourbons 19 (Paris: Editions A. et J. Picard, 1971): 165, discusses the apprenticeship
certificate of the son of Jean Langot dit La Rose to Jean Corbron, joueur d'instrument and
a musician "following the court (suivant la cour)" dated January 25, 1694. This would
support a date in the 1680's for La Rose's appearance at Versailles. Corbron agrees to
provide Langot's son with a violin to earn his living. It is easy to imagine that La Rose
would regard learning the violin as a step up, since the instrument might earn him a place
in the court musical establishment, an option denied to the father.

Illustration 1. "Vielle carrée" after an instrument dated 1774. Copy by Thomas Norwood, Paris.

carrée," generally described today as trapezoidal (see Illustration 1). This trapezoidal instrument was an attempt to reduce the size of the body while keeping the same string length.[11] The three melody strings were tuned in D; one was an octave lower than the other two, with drones in D and A. Thus it was slightly larger than the vielle which later became standard in the eighteenth century (the melody strings of the latter were tuned to G). In spite of later innovations, this shape continued to be used throughout the eighteenth century.[12] It is pictured by Watteau in the second decade of the eighteenth century, in the hands of gentlemen or idealized peasants in rustic settings.[13] The instrument was most likely used at this time to play the bransles and other dances associated with the French countryside.

Some music specifically for this instrument is found in an opéra comique by Jean-Joseph Mouret (1682-1738), *Le Philosophe trompé par la nature*, presented at the Comédie de Saint Jorry in 1725. The final scene of this piece concerns a group of grape harvesters (*vendangeurs*) who make their entrance to the accompaniment of a vielle, bass viol, and continuo (Example 2). They make light of the philosopher's avoidance of the pleasures of life: their ignorance of Latin does not effect their enjoyment

Example 2. Jean-Joseph Mouret, *Le Philosophe trompé par la nature*, "La Feste de village," entrée.

---

[11]Terrasson (1741): 93-96.

[12]Alain Fougerit, "Fabrication des vielles en Normandie au XVIIIe siècle," *Revue Modale* 3 (January, 1983): 6-35, puts forth the hypothesis that this instrument was developed and made primarily by Norman makers. Claude Flagel, "Vielles de Normandie: La 'Terrassonite'!" *Revue Modale* 5 (Fall, 1984): 37-40, challenges this view.

[13]*The Marriage Contract* is one such painting. He also executed a drawing of the hands of a player of this instrument. There is also a painting in the Birmingham Art Museum entitled *Gentleman Playing the Hurdy-Gurdy* which if not by Watteau is at least contemporary with his work.

of eating, drinking, dancing and making love. While the composer is not specific concerning the instrumentation of the following numbers, some would be appropriate for performance with vielle, and others must have been performed on other instruments, since they make use of keys incompatible with the drones. This music is in A major and was composed for a vielle in D-A, probably the trapezoidal instrument. Presumably the presence of the vielle in this scene is justified by its rustic setting. However, the use of the vielle in the first number is anything but rustic: it is treated in an expressive fashion not unlike any other melody instrument (Example 1).

According to Terrasson, this instrument was flawed by its unrefined melody strings, especially the heavy string at the lower octave. Further, the drone strings were so raucous that they drowned out the melody. Terrasson informs us that Henri Bâton, an instrument maker at Versailles, was the first to build a new type of vielle on the backs of old guitars and lutes then going out of fashion and thus sparked the cultivation of the vielle in court circles.[14] This work seems to have taken place between 1716 and 1720. It is important to remember that an already enthusiastic following among the nobility for the vielle already existed, providing the impetus for these improvements. Terrasson also tells us that Bâton shaped the peg box in the manner of the viol and decorated it in a way which made them "pleasing to the ladies" (Illustration 2). In redesigning the peg box in the manner of the viol, an instrument traditionally played by both upper class men and women, he provided the "new" instrument with a link to respectability. The similarities between the vielle and the viol go beyond appearance and involve the sound and technique to be explored later. However, by 1720 the viol was reaching the peak of its popularity and was about to begin a long, slow decline. Thus the similarity in both sound and appearance between these two instruments may have also contributed to the decline of the use of the vielle in sophisticated chamber music in later decades. It must be emphasized that the vielle of Henri Bâton was a new instrument with musical capabilities far beyond those of earlier instruments and it was being used in a way entirely different than it had before. It had an increased range and melody strings which sang above the drones. As a result, the music composed for it was of an experimental nature, as composers explored

---

[14]Terrasson (1741): 96-98. No instruments verifiably built by Henri Bâton survive. Only one instrument built on the back of a guitar has survived. Built by the luthier Jean-Nicolas Lambert, it is number 523 in the catalogue of the Musée du Conservatoire, Paris.

Illustration 2. Pegbox of a vielle by François Feury, c.1740.

the limits of the capabilities of the instrument. Further experiments in improving the instrument continued throughout the eighteenth century.[15]

Considerable attention has been paid to the social position of the instrument in the eighteenth century in academic discussions of the vielle. The view of the instrument as a plaything of wealthy lady amateurs has by extension led to an unfavorable judgement of the music itself without further examination. The value of the music should be judged on its own merits, independent of its social function in the eighteenth century. Nevertheless, it is worthwhile to examine the basis for this stereotype and its limitations before proceeding to a discussion of the intrinsic value of the music.

The view of the role of music in aristocratic life had its roots in humanist formulations of the sixteenth century based on Plato's discussion of the subject in the *Republic*. Simply put, music was regarded as an important social accomplishment as long as it was kept in its place. The result of these views in cultivated musical circles from the sixteenth to the eighteenth century was a spontaneous, simple form of music-making with emphasis placed on the expression of sentiment and a minimum on technical accomplishment. It generally involved the vocal or instrumental performance of simple airs and dances. Technical polish and virtuosity was best left to those of a lower class who made their living through music.

Early in the eighteenth century attitudes toward the appropriate role of music making in aristocratic life began to change. Gentlemen took up the violin, flute, and to a lesser degree the oboe (the musette had become popular among this group in the seventeenth century). These instruments had been previously the province of the professional, because they were difficult to play well, and the types of music composed for these instruments, that is theater and dance music, were likewise left to professional musicians. The appearance of works for solo and continuo, notably the Italian sonatas of Corelli, provided a type of music which encouraged the adoption of these instruments by the upper classes. Further, this music required a degree of accomplishment bordering on the virtuosic, a trait never before associated with the cultivated amateur. The

---

[15]There were too many changes proposed in the eighteenth century to be discussed here. Most involved extending the range (down a fifth or fourth or up by several more notes) or ameliorating the sound. None of these caught on. Various keyboard arrangements, or *vielles organisées* were also proposed, the only successful incarnation of which was the *lyra organizzata* best known for Haydn's music composed for the King of Naples, an enthusiastic player of this instrument.

role which the ladies played in this "new" type of music was that of accompanist, playing the harpsichord or the bass viol. The avoidance of the violin and wind instruments by women in the early part of the eighteenth century was based on the appearance that these instruments presented when played in public. This appearance involved not only the position of the body but bodily movements as well. Playing the flute and oboe required facial distortion, while the violin and musette involved an unsightly flapping of the upper arm in a way that playing the viol did not. In contrast the vielle presented a pleasing appearance in both bodily position and movement and enabled women to play music in the latest style, first as an equal partner in unaccompanied duos and later in the role of soloist. That the new vielle of Bâton was far more suitable for its role in this type of chamber music was of paramount importance. Nevertheless, this preference for the vielle by women did not exclude men from playing the instrument as well.

The spontaneous, simple musical performance of the past coexisted side by side with more virtuosic displays among the upper class throughout the eighteenth century, but not without tension. Diatribes against the aristocratic virtuoso are common. A letter which appeared in the *Mercure de France* in June 1738 enthused over the new interest taken in the violin by the upper classes.

This instrument [the violin] has been ennobled in our own time. It is no longer shameful for honest men to cultivate it and to grant a kind of glory and esteem to those who excel on it, among whom are counted the highest nobles.[16]

An anonymous letter in the *Mercure de France* in August, 1738 concludes its attack on this observation.

Let us indeed leave to those who were born with these great talents the care to cultivate them in preference to all. . . . It can indeed be permitted under normal conditions to devote oneself to music and to instruments to a certain point; that is to say, as much as is necessary

---

[16]Anon., "Memoires pour servir à l'Histoire de la musique vocale et instrumentale," *Mercure de France* (June, 1738): 1110-1118. "Cet instrument a été ennobli de nos jours il n'est plus honteux aux honnêtes gens de le cultiver, et on veut bien accorder une sorte de gloire et de l'estime à ceux qui y excellent, parmi lesquels on peut compter des Seigneurs de la plus grand Elévation, . . ."

to make oneself agreeable in society and to obtain entries into the [social] world, but for the nobility, they must be occupied with a broader outlook. They are accountable to their country, to the names they carry, and to talents of an altogether different importance.[17]

This attitude applies to all instruments, not just the vielle and musette, and it is deeply rooted in the structure of society. As a result of these two eighteenth-century views, two types of music are found for the vielle, arrangements of popular airs and dances and chamber music in the latest style.

Although solo and trio sonatas and concertos requiring great virtuosity on the part of the player were composed from the 1730s to about 1760, the most important activity of most amateur players of the vielle in the eighteenth century was playing popular tunes arranged for the vielle for oneself and one's friends in informal settings. In this respect the vielle may be compared with the parlor piano or harmonium of the next century. Many of these pieces survive in the methods of Boüin and Corrette, manuscript sources, and in numerous collections of the latest melodies from the opéra comique and the most well known composers.[18] By far, the most numerous publications of this type came from Esprit-Philippe (1696-1762) and Nicolas Chédeville (1705-1782), who in addition to arranging popular tunes, published arrangements of violin sonatas and concertos by Dall'Abaco and Vivaldi. Although their works were primarily intended for the musette, they were appropriated by vielle players as well. Recognizing that vielle players constituted a large portion of those who bought his music, Esprit-Philippe presented in his publica-

---

[17]Anon., "Lettre écrite de Paris le 29. juillet 1738 sur les Memoires pour servir à l'histoire de la musique." *Mercure de France* (August, 1738): 1723. "Laissons donc à ceux qui naissent avec ces grands talens, le soin de les cultiver par préférence à tout, et la liberté de se livrer sans reserve à l'espece d'enthousiasme qu'exigent tous les Arts, qui sont du ressort du goût, pour y réüssir superieurement.

"Il peut bien être permis dans un état moyen de s'adonner à la musique, et aux instrumens jusquà un certain point, c'est à-dire, autant qu'il peut être nécessaire pour se rendre agréable dans la Société, et pour se procurer des entrées dans le monde; mais pour les gens du premier ordre, ils doivent être occupés de plus grandes vûës; ils sont comptables à leur Patrie, et aux noms qu'ils portent, de talens d'une toute autre importance."

[18]Françoise Bois-Poteur is indexing these arrangements of airs and dances for vielle and musette. I estimate that there may be as many as 5000 of them.

tions alternate arrangements of airs for vielle and musette (see Chapter 2, Example 1). Pictorial representations of players of the vielle rarely show these subjects with other instruments. For example, Louis Carrogis (1717-1806), known as Carmontelle did a drawing of Madame de Julienne playing the vielle for Madame de Serré (a relative) in 1760.[19] This picture contrasts with many of Carmontelle's other works which show groups of one to three musicians.

The initial popularity of the vielle was given impetus by the devotion of those in the upper ranks of society. From the 1730s into the 1760s it is possible to identify three groups which cultivated the instrument. The first of these were members of the nobility and royal family at Versailles. This is no surprise in that the activities of the maker Henri Bâton were centered there. More specifically, much of this activity centered around the queen Marie Lesczynska, wife of Louis XV.[20] She is often cited as evidence of the social status that the vielle achieved. However, her musical tastes and cultural interests were not as sophisticated as others at court who cultivated a taste for opera. The evidence is particularly damning in that it comes from those close to her whose affection for her was beyond question. Although she loved the vielle, she did not play it very well, and therefore she has been cited as evidence of the lack of seriousness with which the upper class regarded the instrument in the eighteenth century. In fact, she was the perfect noble amateur who played airs and dances as an agreeable pastime. More partisan views leave the impression that the queen represented a cultural backwater in the society of Versailles, and the king abandoned her for the accomplished singer and harpsichordist Madame de Pompadour who pursued the ideal of the noble virtuoso. Nevertheless, the queen invited such virtuosi as M. Danguy to

---

[19]Madame de Julienne had been the wife of the son of Jean de Julienne (1686-1766), director of the Gobelin textile factories and associate of Watteau. Left a widow in 1755, she became associated with the circle of Mme. d'Epinay, one of the most famous hostesses and female literary figures of the period. This drawing is now in the Musée Carnavalet. For further discussion, see Claude Flagel, "La Vielle parisienne sous Louis XV: un modèle pour deux siècles," *Instrumentistes et luthiers parisiens XVIIᵉ-XIXᵉ siècles.* Ed. Florence Gétreau (Paris: Délégation à l'Action Artistique de Paris, 1988): 106-107, 127.

[20]The most detailed source concerning the musical activities of the queen are the memoires that the Duc de Luynes kept between 1735 and 1758. The modern edition fills seventeen volumes, but the musical references have been extracted in *La Musique à la cour de Louis XIV et de Louis XV d'après les Mémoires de Sourches et Luynes 1681-1758.* Norbert Dufourcq, ed. (Paris: Éditions A. & J. Picard, 1970): 53-180.

court where they performed for various members of the royal family, who appeared to receive these concerts with pleasure.[21] After such a performance, it was not uncommon for the queen to play simple duets with these musicians. Another amateur in this circle was the Duchess de Bourgogne, the king's niece. Charles Bâton, son of the maker Henri and a virtuoso and composer, dedicated his collection of suites *La vielle amusante* to her, affirming on the title page that he was her teacher.

A second group of amateurs are to be found among the *noblesse de la robe*, lawyers, judges and tax farmers, who, lacking noble blood, had bought or married their way into the nobility. Lacking the family blood lines which would distinguish them in society, they compensated for a lack of background with a wholehearted pursuit of the arts. Since they were quite wealthy, money was not the restraint that it might have been on many members of the poorer nobility. Many of the published collections of music for the vielle were dedicated to members of this group, who served as patrons as well as amateur players. A number of manuscript collections from their personal libraries survive. Among the most prominent of these amateurs was M. Le Rebours, a member of the Paris Parlement ("conseiller") who patronized the composer-teacher Michon. The character piece *Musette La le Rebours* is found in his first collection, and the composer dedicated his second collection to Le Rebours as well. A large manuscript of dance pieces for vielle and bass from the latter's library is now in the Bibliothèque Nationale.[22] Another amateur player from this group was Madame de Senozan to whom Bâton dedicated his six sonatas, Op.3.[23] A manuscript collection of one-line airs from her library is extant.[24] One of the most important of these amateurs was the financier and musical patron La Pouplinière (1693-1762). An amateur composer and student of Jean-Philippe Rameau, he often sang his own airs while accompanying himself on the vielle or guitar.[25]

A third group which cultivated the vielle was the provincial gentry of

---

[21]Luynes (Dufourcq), p.79 (February 19, 1744), and p.104 (October 23, 1746).

[22]Paris, Bibliothèque Nationale, Vm⁷3643. See Chapter 4.

[23]This dedication mentions that the vielle is one of her occupations without suggesting that she is necessarily capable of playing the sonatas.

[24]Paris, Bibliothèque Nationale, Cons.L.12.867. See Chapter 4.

[25]Georges Cucuel, *La Pouplinière et la musique de chambre au XVIIIᵉ siècle* (Paris: Librairie Fischbacker, 1913. Rpt. New York: Da Capo Press, 1971): 288.

both sexes. With the paucity of music teachers in rural areas or small cities, the vielle was easier to pursue on one's own than, for example, the violin. Arras, Caen, Rheims, Grenoble, Lyon and Toulouse all had luthiers who made vielles and were presumably supported by local activity. A large manuscript prepared for a M. Houe of Toulouse, "conseiller du consul souverain de l'isle Guadeloupe," gives some idea of the types of repertory played outside Paris.[26] M. Houe enjoyed playing the works of all the most famous composers, as well as popular songs and dance tunes. The large majority of these works are for the vielle alone, but there are some for two vielles as well. Nothing of a regional nature is included, for provincial musicians looked to Paris for the latest music.

Fragmentary sources provide additional names of amateurs among these groups who played the vielle. For example, inventories of musical instruments which were confiscated along with other goods during the 1790's from 111 noble households list six which possessed vielles.[27]

Dedications on title pages of the music and the music itself indicate that there were some truly accomplished players among the upper classes in the 1730s and 1740s. It is possible to identify some of these from the dedication pages of music by Boüin, Bâton and other teachers who referred specifically to their dedicatees' musical activities. For example, Michel Corrette dedicated his *Six fantaisies à trois parties* to Monsieur Delpech d'Angerville, Conseiller au Parlement, Marquis de Mereville, clearly a member of the second group. In the dedications he says, "The honor that you do every day to my music by playing it on the vielle, on which you equal the most capable masters, makes me take the liberty of offering to you these fantasies. . . ."[28] While it is generally assumed that these dedications flatter the abilities of the dedicatees, there is no reason

---

[26]Paris, Bibliothèque de l'Arsenal, Ms.2547. See Chapter 4.

[27]A. Bruni, *Un Inventaire sous la terreur*. J. Gallay, ed. (Paris: Georges Chamerot, 1890). The households which possessed vielles are those of Marquis Chabert de Cogolin (1724-1805) who owned two vielles, the Vicomte de Noailles (1756-1804), le Comte de Maillebois (1715-1791), François René Cueu d'Herouville (bourgeois)(executed 1794), the wife of the Marquis Marboeuf (executed 1796), and le Comte de Lowendal (dates unknown). The vielle in the possession of the Comte de Noailles is the instrument originally thought to have belonged to the Princess Adelaïde now in the Paris Conservatory Museum (cat. no.124).

[28]"L'honneur que vous faite tous les jours à ma musique, en l'executant sur la Viele, dont vous égalez nos most habiles Maîtres, me fait prendre la liberté de Vous offrir ces Fantaisies. . . ."

to assume that they did not play well.   Further, it is unlikely that composers would write beyond the abilities of these amateurs if they wished to sell their music.

Another example is the *Pièces de caractère* of Jean-Baptiste Dupuits published in 1741, dedicated to Madame D'Obrien, "Sennora D'onor" to her majesty the Queen of Spain. In the dedication Dupuits says, ". . . the way in which you execute them [the pieces] contributes not a little to the degree of perfection which I have been able to attain." [29]   The first pieces in this collection are grouped into two suites named *La sennora* and the *Amusements de la sennora*. These two suites are technically difficult but musically conventional in contrast to the experimental nature of some of the later pieces in the publication.[30] This evidence indicates that Dupuits worked at composing pleasing works specifically for her and that she was capable of playing some of his most difficult music.

Dupuits and others composed and published music for reasons other than renown or patronage. Their works attracted students who came not only to learn to play the instrument but to learn how to play the music of that particular composer.   In the *avertissements* which precede his publications, Dupuits encourages those who have questions about how to play certain passages to visit him, and he gives the days when he can be found at home (see Appendix).

Further impetus to the popularity of the vielle was given by the appearance of virtuosos such as Charles Bâton and M. Danguy. Little is known about these two, but Charles Bâton seems to have spent most of his time in court circles at Versailles, while Danguy was mostly associated with events in Paris.[31] Accounts of their playing are favorable, even from those who had no great love of the instrument. Danguy is most often described as performing duos with a musette player Colin Charpentier,

---

[29]Dupuits, *Pièces de caractère*, Avertissement, ". . . la façon dont vous les executes [!] ne contribuent pas peu a[!] leurs donner le degré de perfection que je n'ay pû atteindre."

[30]A more complete discussion of the music in this collection is found in conjunction with that of Dupuit's other works.

[31]A decision following a lawsuit filed against Danguy and a Mme. Soygeuze by the famous luthier Jean-Nicolas Lambert dated September 13, 1746 is bound in the back of a copy of the Ballard *Pièces choisies pour la vielle à l'usage des commençants* found in the Newberry Library, Chicago. Lambert sued for the price of a vielle and costs and won. The circumstances surrounding the suits are not explained. A likely possibility is that Mme. Soygeuze as a student of Danguy bought an instrument from Lambert on credit and then failed to pay.

who was also a singer.   They were much in demand and played on occasion for the queen at Versailles, but they also took part in performances at the Concerts Spirituels.   In 1733, for the wedding supper of the grand daughter of the financier Samuel Bernard with the Marquis de Mirepoix, one of the many cases of money marrying position, Danguy and Charpentier performed a concert of works composed specifically for the occasion by Jean-Philippe Rameau.[32]

From the inception of the Concerts Spirituels in 1728, it was customary to perform suites of noëls with the orchestra at the performances which took place on December 24 and 25.   In 1728, the musette made its appearance, and in 1732 Danguy and Charpentier performed arrangements of noëls by Michel Corrette with the orchestra.[33]   These were so well received that this performance became an annual tradition, lasting until at least 1743.[34]   In 1742 and 1743, Danguy and Charpentier performed noëls with the orchestra between movements of the motet *Fugit nox* by Joseph Bodin de Boismortier (1689-1755).[35]

Both Danguy and Charpentier appear to have had some involvement with the Théâtres de la Foire. A piece described as "air de la Comédie Italienne de Danguy" is extant.[36]   Charpentier made his acting debut in *La Tante rival* in 1729.[37]   Danguy seems to have had a long career of performing and teaching, since he may have been active as late as 1785.[38]

---

[32]As quoted in Cucuel, p.313, "Au milieu du souper les sieurs Charpentier et Dangoy [!], célèbres concertants, l'un sur la musette, l'autre sur la vielle, vinrent au milieu du fer à cheval exécuter des morceaux que Rameau avait composés exprès pour cette occasion."

[33]Michel Corrette published at least five concertos de noëls of which only two mention the vielle specifically on the title page, but three are in fact playable on the instrument (see Chapter 3).

[34]Danguy and Charpentier are not listed by name after 1733, but the repertory in subsequent performances remained the same, and it is most likely that they continued their performances.

[35]This motet is lost. It seems likely that Boismortier made the arrangements of noëls performed on these occasions. Although he published one concerto de noëls in 1737, only one part survives.

[36]Paris, Bibliothèque de l'Arsenal, Ms.2547, p.38.

[37]Clifford R. Barnes, "Instruments and Instrumental Music at the 'Théâtres de la foire' (1697-1762)" *Recherches* 5 (1965): 156.

[38]Anon., *Tablettes de renommée des musiciens, auteurs, compositeurs, virtuoses, amateurs et*

While the vielle, in the words of Boüin, might not have been "to the taste of everyone," modern scholars have quoted eighteenth-century attacks on the vielle, while ignoring their context.[39] A fuller discussion of the two most important of these can demonstrate more clearly the attitudes toward the instrument which sparked these polemics. The first was published in August of 1738 in the *Mercure de France* in response to a letter discussing the state of music.[40] After praising the violin as an instrument worthy of study, the author, as an aside, announces that the only instrument not worthy of attention is the vielle which should be returned to the blind men and cafés from which it came, because its continual blaring is an affront to sensitive ears. The diatribe ends with a denunciation of the musette as well.[41] After attacking the current vogue for the aristocrat to play the virtuoso violinist, he offers generally negative judgements on many aspects of contemporary music. For example, the difficulties of Rameau's music come up for some heavy criticism.[42]

The same conservatism is present in a far more substantial and interesting attack found in a pamphlet published anonymously by François Campion (c.1686-1748) entitled *Lettre de Monsieur l'Abbé Carbasus, à Monsieur de *** auteur du Temple de Goust sur la mode des instruments de musique* in 1739.[43] Campion was the finest guitarist of his time, a

---

maîtres de musique vocale et instrumentale, les plus connus en chaque genre . . . pour servir à l'Almanach-Dauphin (Paris, 1785), mentions a Danguy active as a teacher of the vielle, but this may have been a son.

[39]Boüin, p.13. See Lindeman, pp.28-35, for a number of other disputes concerning the musette and vielle. Also see Leppert, p.105.

[40]Anon., "Lettre écrite de Paris le 29, Juillet 1738, sur les Memoires pour servir à l'Histoire de la Musique," *Mercure de France* August, 1738, pp.1721-1732.

[41]Lettre, p.1722, ". . . mais on pourroit sans inconvenient pour le bon goût, releguer la Vielle aux Ginguettes, et l'abandonner aux Aveugles; car, n'en deplaise aux Danguis, et aux Belles qui s'y sont adonnées depuis quelques années, c'est un Instrument si borné et son cornement perpetuel est si désagréable pour des oreilles délicates, qu'il devroit être proscrit sans misericorde; peut s'en faut que j'en dise autant de la Musette qui ne peut être admise raisonnablement que dans une Fête champêtre."

[42]Lettre, p.1728, ". . . l'on court risque de donner, comme a fait R*** dans le bizarre souvent outré; car le mérite de toute espece de Musique ne consiste nullement dans la difficulté de l'exécution; . . ."

[43]See also Bröcker, pp.410-413 for a somewhat different summary of this pamphlet.

theorist, and a composer of considerable talent. Voltaire's part-poem, part-essay *Temple de Goût* was published in 1732 (revised 1733). It is an attack on poor taste in all the arts. Voltaire describes a concert given at the house of an *"homme de la robe"* who has more money than taste (a contemporary stereotype) and shows great enthusiasm for both French and Italian styles without understanding the difference between them. In Campion's *Lettre*, the fictitious Abbé attends this concert with Voltaire.[44] Also in attendance is a widowed marquise, a friend of the Abbé who is a talented harpsichordist. The catalogue of her musical accomplishments is truly formidable. She can play Couperin and the two-manual pieces of Rameau. She owns and has presumably studied Rameau's *Traité d'harmonie* and Campion's own theoretical treatise *La Régle de l'octave*. She can transpose at sight a half step lower or higher. She is thoroughly familiar with both French and Italian styles and can improvise variations and three-, four- and five-part fugues and double fugues. After Voltaire leaves, the concert concludes with a surprise: a trio consisting of a musette, a vielle, and a bassoon performs.[45] Carbasus is disgusted by the dissonance and "confusion" which seems to characterize this music, but to his horror, the marquise is enraptured by what she hears. The next day he visits her and finds the performer of the previous night hired as her vielle teacher. Not entirely convinced that she should abandon the harpsichord for the vielle, she asks the vielle teacher if this would be a wise decision and if she is in fact suited to play the instrument. This question stimulates a long lecture from the vielle teacher which includes a long, nonsensical history of the instrument, much like that which Terrasson would publish two years later. He goes on to criticize the limitations of every other instrument and their unsuitability for women. Campion cleverly has the vielle teacher espouse these attitudes which undoubtedly were widely held, so that his eloquence is quite seductive. The author then plays his hand, and the real reason behind this treatise is revealed. The marquise tells the vielle teacher that she has an ornate and very expensive guitar which the teacher advises her should be made into a vielle. When the marquise hesitates, the vielle teacher says, "Ah, Madame! your scruples astonish me. . . . You are indeed not informed that

---

[44]It is surprising that Campion picks the character of an abbé for his protagonist since Voltaire's work begins with an anticlerical attack.

[45]This is the ensemble depicted on the cover of Michel Corrette's *Fantaisies à trois parties* (c.1731). Corrette includes in this work pieces for musette, vielle and bass which could be played by such an ensemble. See p.37.

it is the only use today for theorbos, lutes and guitars. These gothic and despised instruments are as a last resort turned into vielles: that is their grave." [46]

There follows a discussion of the decline of the guitar since the great old days of Louis XIV. This sets the stage for an exhortation on the part of the vielle teacher to follow current fashion at all costs, for to go against fashion is to go against nature. ". . . Fashion is the daughter of novelty, adopted and cherished by persons with good taste, who do not look at things as they should be, but as they are." [47] The marquise is thoroughly convinced by this argument, but Carbasus saves her at the last minute and reveals the fallacy in the vielle teacher's philosophy.

Campion, whose career had suffered from the decline in interest in the guitar in spite of his considerable abilities, must have seen himself as the victim of fickle fashion. The destruction of guitars and lutes for the purpose of making the new instrument designed by Henri Bâton must have truly rankled. It is little wonder that he chose the vielle as a symbol for the great tragedy of his life.

The vielle would eventually suffer from the changing fortunes of fashion and musical style as well. When Terrasson published his treatise in 1741, he concluded it on an optimistic note. "In a word, the prodigious quantity of new music which is composed every day for it: the increase in ability that our vielle teachers acquire themselves by continual practice: all assures us that the reign of this instrument will endure." [48] In 1768 he replaced this passage with a rather gloomy one. "But in spite of all that [improvements, music], the vicissitude of human things which influence instruments as they do everything else in life have caused a bit of a decline in the [popularity of] vielles and musettes, especially since clarinets, horns, and other loud instruments have expelled theorbos, lutes and bass viols which (in the feeling of all true connoisseurs) were with the

---

[46]Campion, p.18, "Eh, Madame! votre scrupule m'étonne! reprit le Maître. Vous n'êtes pas informée que c'est le seul usage que l'on fait aujourd'hui des Théorbes, des Luths, & des Guitares. Ces Instrumens gothiques & méprisables sont en dernier ressort métamorphosés en Vielles; c'est-là leur tombeau."

[47]Campion, p.41, ". . . la Mode est fille de la Nouveauté, adoptée & chérie des personnes de bon Goût, qui ne regardent point les choses comme elles devroient être, mais comme elles font."

[48]Terrasson (1741): 104, "En un mot, la prodigieuse quantité de Musique nouvelle que l'on compose pour elle: l'augmentation d'habilité que nos Maîtres de Vielle acquierent eux-mêmes par une pratique continuelle: tout nous assure que le Régne de cet Instrument sera durable."

harpsichord the only instruments capable of supporting and nourishing the harmony." [49]

Terrasson was a champion of the virtuoso-oriented music composed by Bâton and others and does not mention the airs and other popular tunes arranged for the instrument. Classified with the older instruments, vielle and its concerted music which seemed so new in the 1730's were now looked on as outmoded. While the popularity of the vielle as an instrument for chamber music was in decline, the general popularity of the instrument for the playing of popular airs and dances was as stable as ever and remained so throughout the century. Although the instrument may have been abandoned by court circles after 1760, it had permeated all levels of society, even the street performers populating the boulevards and the walks of the Palais Royale. In the words of one writer, "The fashion for the vielle was not the concern of the nobility alone. Bit by bit it entered the plan of the general culture." [50]   As a result, the French Revolution was perhaps less disruptive to the fortunes of the instrument than has been implied.

How large a part of the musical scene was devoted to playing, performing and composing for the vielle in the eighteenth century? In spite of the obvious difficulties in answering such a question, a few statistics might provide at least an approximate answer. A tabulation of the contents of the music catalogues of Parisian publishers shows that of the 1649 musical editions and methods available in 1742, at the highpoint of the instrument's popularity, 113 titles were listed for the musette and vielle.[51] In 1751, out of a total of 2348 titles, 156 were listed for these two instruments. Of the 489 composers active between 1730 and 1760, whose works were published in Paris, at least 56 composed music for the musette

---

[49]Terrasson (1768): 254, "Mais malgré tout cela, la vicissitude des choses humaines, qui influe sur les instruments comme sur toutes les autres choses de la vie, a fait un peu tomber les musettes et les vielles; surtout depuis que les clarinettes, les cors de chasse et autres instruments bruyants ont fait expulser des concerts les théorbes, luts et basses de viole qui cependant (au sentiment de tous les vrais connoisseurs) estoient avec le clavessin les seuls instruments capables d'entretenir et de nourrir l'Harmonie." This passage is also quoted by Bricqueville, p.44, who was unaware of the 1741 edition of Terrasson.

[50]"La mode de la vielle ne concerne pas seulement la noblesse, elle s'inscrit peu à peu au programme de culture génerale;. . ." Jean-François Chassaing, *La vielle et les luthiers de Jenzat* (Combronde: Aux Amoureux de Science, 1987): 13.

[51]Anik Devriès, *Édition et commerce de la musique gravée à Paris dans la première moitié du XVIIe siècle* (Geneva: Éditions Minkoff, 1976): 74-75.

and vielle. As mentioned earlier, 6 out of 111 families owned vielles in Bruni's list of confiscated instruments. From these fragmentary numbers it would seem safe to say that between five and ten percent of the musical activity was devoted to playing the vielle. While this does not seem high, in the world of amateur music making where the large majority was vocal, the vielle falls behind only the violin, flute, and harpsichord in popularity.

The romanticized transformation of the vielle player Fanchon, the street performer whose virtue triumphs over adversity, became one of the most popular subjects for the stage in the early nineteenth century, reawakening an interest in the vielle and the republication of Corrette's method in the early nineteenth century.[52]   Nevertheless, activities involving the instrument gradually shifted away from Paris itself. It was played in Normandy and in regions of central France, the Auvergne, Berry, Bourbonnais, the Morvan, and Périgord. In the early nineteenth century, the town of Jenzat near Vichy became the center of vielle construction for the region. The most prominent of these luthiers, the Pajots, had been minor government officials in the eighteenth century with distant ties to the French court.[53] The first instruments made by them were modelled on those of the eighteenth century. Their clients came from all classes. Some were established middle class from the surrounding towns, who ordered highly decorated instruments. Others were members of the peasantry. The instruments were played outdoors for weddings and town gatherings including dances, as well as in taverns, and these new requirements necessitated bigger instruments which produced more sound. The types of music and playing styles changed as well.

A decline in interest in regional music in the twentieth century almost destroyed this tradition. A reawakening of interest in the 1960's and 1970's, however, has revived interest in this music and the instruments associated with it including the vielle. Enough players survived from the early part of the twentieth century to establish a continuous tradition. Georges Simon and Gaston Rivière, among others, have taught hundreds of students the playing styles of nineteenth-century traditional music. A new generation of virtuoso players has refined the technique of playing

---

[52]The list of plays and operas based on Fanchon is too lengthy to give here. For a fairly complete list, see, John Ralyea, *The Shepherd's Delight*, 2nd ed. (Chicago: The Author, 1988): 125-192. Many of these stage works have parts for the vielle. Most notable among these are Luigi Cherubini's *Les deux journées* (1800) and Gaetano Donizetti's opera *Linda di Chamonix* (1842). The latter contains music for the vielle, but the former does not.

[53]Chassaing, pp.13-15, traces the origins of the Pajot family.

traditional music in a manner more precise than those of preceding generations. Valentin Clastrier has extended the possiblities of the instrument, developing an avant garde musical style out of traditional origins. The instrument itself continues to evolve, as luthiers experiment with different body shapes and gadgetry which produce different sounds and easier tuning.[54] The emphasis on technique and attempts to extend the possiblities of the instrument have redefined traditional music in a twentieth-century manner. This movement has many analogies with the same trend in America where the interest in traditional music has led to creative activities far removed from their original roots.

But current interest in the vielle has not so far extended to include the eighteenth-century repertory. In the recent past, this music was viewed as "elitist," the very antipathy of what many who were interested in traditional music valued. Further, the activities and skills required for folk music are entirely different. A good ear for style and for picking up tunes, as later chapters in this book will show, is only the beginning for the mastering of the eighteenth-century repertory. There is little communal in the activities related to learning this literature. Unlike traditional music where people gather in large groups to play in unison, as with any "classical" repertory, much time has to be spent alone in a practice room.

This is not to say that the players of the vielle have been unaware or totally uninterested in the eighteenth century. At least as early as the 1880's groups of *instruments anciens* presented concerts in Paris including the vielle. Eugène de Bricqueville mentions a vielle player Laurent Grillet who participated in these concerts.[55] De Bricqueville himself was the leader of a group *La Couperin* which specialized in eighteenth-century French music on period instruments at the beginning of this century. As part of this group he performed the most significant repertory for the vielle. Although De Bricqueville, and presumably Grillet, had read the eighteenth-century treatises and thus knew about as much about performance practice as we do today, they felt it necessary to make considerable compromises so as not to offend audiences. Grillet completely eliminated the drones, and De Bricqueville used them only for dance movements.

The pioneering recordings of Michelle Fromenteau in the 1970's of this repertory alerted people to its tunefulness and appeal. Mme. Fromenteau,

---

[54]For a description of some of these new instruments, see Pascal Lefeuvre, "La Vielle à roue. 800 ans d'évolution (2ème partie)," *Trad Magazine* 29 (juillet/août 1993): 8-11.

[55]Eugène de Bricqueville, *Notice sur la vielle* (Paris: Rpt. La Flûte de Pan, 1980): 52-53.

however, made her recordings on a nineteenth-century instrument of the Pajots in company with other musicians using modern instruments.[56] In the late seventies and early eighties Claude Flagel made recordings using an eighteenth-century instrument together with musicians playing period instruments. In the ten years since these recordings, more and more of the eighteenth-century repertory has been recorded. This literature does not yield its secrets easily through the study of scores, and therefore a true evaluation of the musical quality of the music for the vielle will come only through repeated hearings.

---

[56]For a discography of eighteenth-century repertory as of 1981, see John Ralyea, *Shepherd's Delight*, pp.58-59.

CHAPTER TWO

THE MUSIC

General Stylistic Features of French Music

In the seventeenth century, a well-established tradition of vocal chamber music permeated the upper classes. The *air*, a solo song accompanied by the lute, or later the harpsichord, and bass viol was the most frequent form of home entertainment. Instrumental chamber music consisted mainly of solo works for harpsichord, lute, and viol (unaccompanied). The publication of the solo part book of the *Pièces à une et à deux violes* in 1686 followed by its continuo part book, three years later, was the first instrumental solo-bass collection published in France. All of the above mentioned vocal and instrumental works had one element in common not found in the music of other countries: the solo part was sufficient unto itself and could be performed without accompaniment. Later in the eighteenth, when instrumental solo-bass music became common, this feature was retained. The bass part, although desirable for the full realization of the work, was an addition. This feature contrasted with the solo-bass sonata in Italy, where the bass was an integral part of the work. The independence of the solo part is particularly true of the solo-bass music for the vielle. The independence of the solo part made the bass part more independent as well, since its accompanimental role was less important. As a result, bass lines can be extremely florid, highlighting and commenting on the gestures of the upper part. Thus the way is paved for a truly conversational style, one of the features of the *style galant*.

The appearance of the Italian solo sonata and concerto in France in the last decade of the seventeenth century and the first two decades of the eighteenth resulted in a variety of hybrid types of chamber music often, but not always, called sonatas. They combined traditional French materials, mainly associated with the dance, with features associated with the Italian genres. Academic discussions of this phenomenon often center around Couperin's conscious combinations known as *les goûts réunis*, but his efforts represent only a beginning. But by the 1730s and 1740s, when most of the music for the vielle was composed, the features of both French and Italian styles had been fully internalized, so that composers could unself-consciously mingle the two. While this is true in a general sense of all the chamber music composed in these decades, composers for the vielle and musette mingled these two styles in unique ways. In the following discussion of individual composers of music for the vielle, several examples of this mingling will be examined.

Eighteenth-century French chamber music was to some degree independent of the medium for which it was composed. One finds on the title pages of most works a variety of possible instrumentation, for example, works for flute which can be played on the violin or oboe. While some have dismissed this feature as a blatant attempt at commercialization, this is, in fact, a product of the nature of the music itself. The emphasis in French music was always on the melody, a feature which found its origins in the seventeenth-century *air*: even figuration was basically melodic (and thus singable). Nevertheless, certain instruments realized the intentions of the composer more fully than others, and the lists of alternate instruments on title pages were arranged in a descending order of desirability.[1] For example, Charles Bâton's first work is a set of duets entitled *Premier ouevre contenant trois suites pour deux vielles, muzettes, flûtes traversières, flûtes à bec, et hautbois avec la basse continue.* Clearly the work is primarily intended for the vielles. That was the composer's instrument; however, the range of the pieces allows for the possibility of performance on the musette, a drone instrument like the vielle.[2] There are dynamic indications possible on the vielle but not realizable on the musette, but they can be ignored if necessary. Further, there may be movements which contain notes above the range of the musette. These passages must be transposed down, or discarded as unplayable (some publications give alternate passages for musette and vielle when this happens). The duos also fall within the range of three melody instruments, transverse flute, recorder and oboe. These three may be arranged in order of popularity. The effect of the drones is lost with these

---

[1] For a fuller discussion of this subject, see Robert A. Green, "Title Pages of Eighteenth-Century French Chamber Music as a Guide to Performance Practice," *The Courant* I, no.4 (1983): 21-25.

[2] The range of the vielle was two chromatic octaves (g'-g''') whereas the range of the musette was a little over an octave and a half (f#'-d''').

alternates, and, therefore, they are of lesser desirability. It is thus possible by this analysis of title page and contents to identify those works intended primarily for the vielle.

Stylistic Features of the Music for Vielle

The music for the vielle may be divided into two categories: arrangements of popular airs and dances in solo, solo-bass, and duo, and concerted works in the mainstream of the latest France and Italian styles. The former category is the most numerous and grew out of the seventeenth-century tradition of performing airs as instrumental works. The latter category was a much newer style was pursued by a smaller part of the musical population. The numerous publications of the Chédevilles contain hundreds of these arrangements. *Le Queux du chat pour la vièle* is one of these (Example 1).[3] It comes from a collection of melodies without bass and designed to be performed alone. It exceeds the range of the musette with the addition of the E flat for which an alternate arrangement transposed down is included later in the publication. Although it is for the most part diatonic, grating A flats and passing dissonances are present which may relate to the reaction of a cat having its tail pulled.

Example 1. Esprit-Philippe Chédeville, "La Queue du chat pour la vielle," from *II⁰ recueil de contredanses ajustés pour les musettes et vièles*, p.15.

---

[3]This piece will be familiar to most readers as the Tambourin in E minor found in Jean-Philippe Rameau's *Pièces de clavessin* (1724). He later used it again in an orchestrated version in *Les Fêtes d'Hebe* (first performed May 21, 1739). This work may have originated in Rameau's work for the Comédie Italien in the 1720's and may be an original melody by him or an arrangement of a preexistent melody. Chédeville's failure to attribute this to Rameau may be evidence that it was not originally composed by the latter, since Chédeville generally provided the original stage work or composer when known. The title itself ("The Cat's Tail") has no association with any context involving Rameau's use of the melody and therefore suggests that the melody had a life of its own.

The concerted music for the vielle is similar to those found in the chamber music for all instruments in this period. Multi-movement works include solo-bass sonatas and suites of dance movements or character pieces. The unaccompanied duo for two vielles, consisting primarily of suites of dance movements, is an important part of the repertory. Often the distinction between the sonata and the suite is minimal. The sonata begins with a lyrical slow movement followed by a fast movement, which may be fugal, in a binary or through-composed form. The following movements are usually dance movements, with an occasional movement labelled "air" or "aria," depending on the "Italian" content. The suite begins also with a slow movement, but this is followed immediately by dance movements. French overtures, as a means of establishing the "Frenchness" of the work, frequently occur at the beginnings of these suites.[4]

One type of piece has unique features associated only with the music for the vielle and musette, the trio for two drone instruments or one drone instrument and one melody instrument, and basso continuo. These works

---

[4]For example, the composer Michon, to be discussed below, consciously maintained this distinction.

are rarely named "sonate en trio", because they rarely exhibit the characteristics common to that genre.   Instead, these works are called "gentilesse" (by Boismortier) or "fête rustique" (by Naudot), or a host of other nondescript titles. They exhibit a ritornello form and other concerto-like features.   At the beginning of these works a ritornello theme is presented by both instruments playing in unison or in thirds with simple counterpoint, followed by a series of solos for each instrument which are separated by ritornello material. While the unison ritornello may seem a bit rudimentary, the drones of the instruments provide a filler which gives it an orchestral effect. In the works for two vielles or musettes and bass, the harmonic plan is necessarily restricted, and the contrast between the solos is based on the material. In the works where a drone instrument and melody instrument are contrasted, the solos for the melody instrument provide modulations not possible against the drones.   Further contrast is provided by the ranges and types of figuration most suitable for the different instruments.

As implied in the above discussion, composing for a drone instrument may involve some harmonic limitations. Even so, these are few, and the means by which composers work around them is a study in itself. Composers were well aware of these limitations. The problem with drones is the establishment of subsidiary keys beyond tonic and dominant. In most forms commonly found in the music of this time, binary and rondeau forms, this is not a serious problem in that tonic and dominant are, of course, the keys of necessity and readily available. It is a greater problem in ritornello forms, as indicated above.[5] Some composers, the Chédevilles or Michel Corrette, deal with the problem by simply avoiding anything beyond the prolongation of the secondary dominant. Others, however, have a greater tolerance for dissonance. Michon, for example, uses on occasion the minor subdominant, which results in grinding A

Example 2. Michon, *Amusemens de chambre*, Suite en duo, ariette, mineur, mm.15-19.

---

[5]See the *Avertissement* for Dupuits' *Sonates pour un clavecin et une vièle* in the Appendix.

flats against the C-G drones (Example 2).

Some composers avoid establishing dissonant keys by encompassing the notes of the chord and the drones in some type of seventh or ninth. The dominant of the subdominant is a particularly rich chord on a drone instrument, since the B flat in the melody blends well with the C-G drones (Example 3).

Example 3. Jacques-Christophe Naudot, Sonata in C Major, Op.14, no.1, 2nd mov't., Allegro, mm.66-70.

The resolution to the subdominant can be very dissonant, but the A is often treated as part of a ninth chord which includes C and G. Composers have a greater tolerance for the dissonance created by passing chords, particularly when they occur over a pedal. Below is an example from the works of Dupuits.

Example 4. Jean-Baptiste Dupuits. *Pièces de caractère*, "L'Unique", mm.202-211 (Drones G-g-d').

A systematic statement of the tonal system associated with the vielle is found in Toussaint Bordet's method.[6]   Given that the most common activity for the player of the vielle was the performance of the latest tunes, Bordet felt that the most important musical skill for the player of this instrument was arrangement and transposition. He therefore laid out in systematic detail what was and what was not permissible harmonically for the instrument.

It is necessary to observe that the airs which are transposed in these two modes [C major-minor and G major-minor] for the aforementioned instruments [musette and vielle] must modulate in the major key only to the dominant, and, in passing, to the subdominant. With regard to the minor mode, airs can modulate not only to the dominant and to the subdominant, but also to the mediant [relative major] and the minor sixth, as well as the seventh [dominant of the relative major], but it is necessary in this case that the passage not last longer than a measure or two, and that it must be softened and treated with art. Otherwise it would be hard on the ear, because the [drone] strings or bourdons, which sound continually the fifth and the tonic note, would become foreign strings in the new key and would form without ceasing badly placed dissonances which would be unbearable if the passage lasted a long time.[7]

---

[6][Toussaint] Bordet, *Méthode raisonnée pour apprendre la musique d'une façon plus claire et plus précise à laquelle on joint l'étendue de la flûte traversière, du violon, du pardessus de viole, de la vielle et de la musette, leur accord, quelques observations sur la touche desdits instruments et des leçons simples, mésurées et variées, suivies d'un recueil d'airs en duo faciles et connus pour la plus-part.* Paris [1755].

[7]Bordet *Méthode*, p.13-14, "Il faut observer, que les airs que l'on transposent dans ces deux tons pour lesdits instruments ne doivent moduler dans la Mode Majeur, qu'à la Dominante & en passant à la Sous Dominante. A l'égard du Mode Mineur, les Airs peuvent moduler, non seulement aussi à la Dominante & sous Dominante, mais encore à la Mediante & à la 6te mineure ainsi qu'à la 7e; mais il faut dans ce cas, que le passage ne dure pas plus d'une mesure ou deux seulement, & qu'il soit adouci & fait avec art; car autrement il seroit dure à l'oreille, parce que les Cordes ou Bourdons, qui continuellement sonnent l'accord de 5te. & fondamentale du premier ton, deviendroit des cordes étrangeres au nouveau ton, & formeroit sans cesse des dissonances mal placées, qui seroient insuportables si le trait duroit longtemps."
   Paris, Bibliothèque Nationale, Ms. Cons. Rés.1177, f.11[r], is much more restrictive on the tonal possiblities. He specifically rejects the use of E-flat major, F minor, and B-flat major in C minor.

The composer's ability to create harmonic variety while deemphasizing the dissonance which results is, as Bordet implies, the measure of his art. Nevertheless, that the harmonic limitations and passing dissonance struck "delicate ears" as a distinguishing, and sometimes unpleasant feature of this music is evident from attacks on the musette and vielle and from music which was composed in imitation of it.[8]

It is possible to divide composers who published music for the vielle into two categories. Those who composed primarily for the vielle were often virtuosi or teachers of the instrument. Foremost among them were Bâton, Dupuits, Ravet, Michon, and Boüin. In general they were not individually prolific, publishing only one to four collections of music each. To the second category belong those composers who wrote for other instruments as well. These included Boismortier, Corrette, and Naudot. To these must be added Louis-Gabriel Guillemain (1705-1770), one of the most brilliant composers of the period, whose works for vielle and musette have, unfortunately, not survived.[9] They often brought to their compositions for the vielle a highly polished compositional style but often less of an understanding of the idiomatic and technical features of the instrument. The latter group of composer are discussed first.

Joseph Bodin de Boismortier

Boismortier's reputation as an early eighteenth-century composer of chamber music needs no lengthy discussion here. Discussions of his music, however, have generally ignored his substantial contribution to the music for musette and vielle. Boismortier's music for these instruments can be divided into three categories: (1) unaccompanied duos for two vielles or musettes, or drone instrument and melody instrument; (2) trios for two drone instruments or drone instrument and melody instrument

---

[8]François Campion, *Lettre de Monsieur l'Abbé Carbasus, à Monsieur de *** auteur du temple du goust sur la mode des instruments de musique*. Paris: 1738, p.10, "Que peut-on penser du goût de plusieurs Symphonistes, qui, loin de refuser de concerter avec ces Instruments, se confondent volontiers avec le cornement perpetuel de leurs insuportables Bourdons?" (What can one think of the taste of many symphonists, who, far from refusing to perform with these instruments [musette and vielle], mingle themselves willingly with the perpetual blaring of unbearable drones?") The author goes on at length concerning the confusion of the melody which results from drones.

[9]See Chapter 4, Works Not Located, for the titles of his two collections. Over twenty per cent of the music for these instruments has been lost.

and bass; and (3) solo-bass works.   For the most part, Boismortier composed in a way which did not differentiate between vielle and musette, although in a number of works, the musette is clearly preferred. This may be a result of his general preference for wind instruments. Such a work is his cantata *Hilas*.

His duos are the slightest of his works (and today the most played). They are among the first works composed for the vielle and musette, and do little to exploit the distinctive features of these instruments. Of most interest is his last collection in this category *Les loisirs du Bercail* for musette or vielle and violin. Throughout the six suites (or "loisirs") the violin stays low in its range, often providing a florid bass or imitative part. In the latter case, the effect is not unlike that of a Bach invention. The dance titles often hide a small joke, for example, the *IVe Loisir* contains a gigue masquerading as a gavotte (Example 5).

The *IIIe Loisir* contains a movement labelled "Pesamment" which looks as rhythmically square as any from the period, but appearances are

Example 5. Joseph Bodin de Boismortier, *Les Loisirs du Bercail*, IVe Loisir, Gavotte, mm.1-20.

deceiving: Portions of it are offset by half a measure creating an off-balance effect.

The bulk of the trios are collections entitled "gentilesse". Their general concertolike characteristics have been discussed above. They must have been very popular, since there were four collections of them, one of which does not survive. Also of interest in this category are the *Balets [!] de village en trio*, Op.52. These works are extended single movements consisting of short sections in different dance tempos and rhythms. Within a short space of time, the composer goes for the ultimate in contrast.

The six solo-bass sonatas, Op.72, are among the composer's finest works. They date from a period when Boismortier turned to the composition of works for a single instrument, eschewing the undifferentiated style which allowed performance on a variety of different instruments. Collections from this period include the *Pièces de clavecin*, Op.59, and the six solo-bass sonatas for the pardessus de viole, Op.61. That these publications are rare is an indication that they were not very popular. The six sonatas for the vielle are unique in the composer's oeuvre in that they fully exploit the vielle in a way which precludes satisfactory performance on other instruments. These works are short: "miniature" would not be an inappropriate term for some of them. Four of them are three-movement works; the other two have four. All contain an "Aria" as a middle movement and five of the six end with dance movements, two with gigues, two with gavottes, and one with minuets. Sonata No.2 is among the most interesting composed for this instrument. All of its three movements are related thematically by the opening gesture. It is a highly dramatic work and unrelievedly dark in that the work remains in C minor throughout. The second movement is of the type which would later be called "romanza" with a stormy middle section. As with all these sonatas, it uses the entire two-octave range of the instrument, but it saves the highest notes for a climax near the end of the third movement.

Michel Corrette

Early in his career, Corrette was much taken with Vivaldi and composed concertos with a singlemindedness unique to French composers. Corrette composed twenty-three concertos or concerto-like pieces which can be played on the vielle or the musette, the only other works being a

Illustration 3. Michel Corrette, *Fantaisies à trois parties*, title page (© cliché Bibliothèque Nationale, Paris).

suite for solo-bass published as Op.5.[10] Of these concertos, seventeen can be played on vielle or musette with two violins and bass. Like Boismortier, Corrette composed in a style which did not differentiate between the two drone instruments. In fact, all of these concerted works were probably intended for musette, for beneath the title page, the parts are labelled "musette or flute" or "musette or violin" or some variant. This preference for the musette in an orchestral setting is natural in that the musette was an established member of the French orchestra.[11] Nevertheless, these works for the most part work well on the vielle, and the dynamic markings can be realized only on the latter instrument. Eleven of these concertos were designated concertos comiques, because they were first performed at the Opéra Comique. Many of these works (but not all) quote popular or folk tunes referred to in subtitles. Among these, Concerto III *Le Margoton* is unique in the repertory in its scoring for three musettes or vielles and bass. The two lowest instruments function as ripieno while the first part is the true soloist. The latter contains passages which are quite difficult on these instruments. In addition, Corrette composed several Christmas concertos which are arrangements of well known noëls. It is known that these were performed on the vielle at the Concerts Spirituels.

Jacques-Christophe Naudot

Naudot's position as a composer who contributed to the development of the repertory for the flute has been discussed at length. Unfortunately, his compositions for drone instruments have been discussed in the same sources as second-class derivatives of his flute music. The harmonic content is, of course, somewhat restricted by drones, but the added richness compensates for this "shortcoming." Naudot composed one set of duos, two sets of unaccompanied trios, two sets of accompanied trios, a set of six solo-bass sonatas and a set of six concertos. All of these works, with the exception of the sonatas and concertos, are composed in an undifferentiated style which makes them eminently playable on both musette and vielle. The duos, suites of dances and character pieces called

---

[10]For further discussion of these works, see Robert A. Green, "Eighteenth-Century French Chamber Music for the vielle," *Early Music* 15, no.4 (Nov. 1987): 470-471.

[11]The role of the musette in the French opera orchestra is a subject which has hitherto received little attention. For a brief discussion of this subject, see Lindemann, "Pastoral instruments," pp.123-131.

the *Babioles* ("trifles"), are more harmonically varied than similar works by Boismortier and others in this genre. The trios, *Les Plaisirs de Champigny* and the *Divertissement champêtre en trio*, for flute, violin, and musette or vielle, are also suites in the French style. They are the only works in the literature for this combination of instruments. They are well worked out in such a way that balance is not a problem and with a variety of textures possible with such a combination of instruments. The six *Fêtes rustiques* are trios for musette or vielle and melody instrument (violin, flute or oboe). They are chamber concertos which exploit the difference between the melody instrument and drone instrument through different types of figuration and the use of various keys for the melody instrument solos where the drone instrument cannot go.[12]

Arguably the preceding sets may have been intended primarily for the musette, but the solo-bass sonatas and concertos are works specifically composed for the vielle. The solo-bass sonatas are straightforward church sonatas identified as such by the opening slow movement and fugal second movement. In typical French fashion, they are followed by movements in the native style. Some of the sonatas are disappointing in their heavy use of sequence and in general lack the imagination which characterizes much of Naudot's other work. The six concertos, Op.17, on the other hand, are among the few works of their type in the repertory and are among the best.[13] They are melodically inventive and offer many expressive opportunities for the solo instrument. They also effectively contrast the solo instrument with the strings. In addition to the solo-tutti passages, there are ensemble passages where the strings and vielle operate as equal partners, often imitatively. Although straightforward musically, there are many technical difficulties which may result from the composer's not playing the instrument himself.

Charles Bâton

Charles Bâton's career as a virtuoso has been discussed above. His four publications, which appeared between 1733 and roughly 1745, comprise

---

[12]Two of the *Fêtes* are unplayable on the vielle, because they have low F sharps found only on the musette.

[13]Three of the six have come into the repertory of recorder players. They have been criticized as being harmonically conservative in relation to other concertos of the period. However, these critics lack any knowledge of the instrument for which the works were originally written.

eight duo suites, six solo-bass suites, two duo sonatas and four solo-bass sonatas. He was not the first to compose music for the vielle, but he was the first to attempt to exploit the full range and expressive possibilities of the instrument, as well as virtuosic features most suitable to the instrument. Occasionally these features seem superimposed on the music and lack a reason for their existence. Bâton's style is thoroughly French, and he is at his best when exploring the dance movements of a suite: on the other hand, his sonatas include few of the Italian characteristics which distinguish that genre. He is particularly adept at creating interesting textures in his works for two vielles with short bits of imitation and interchange.

Example 6.   Charles Bâton, Sonata Op.5, no.5 for two vielles, 2ᵉ Gigue, mm.29-33.

Bâton's rhythmic sense in his dance movements is subtle and not without its difficulties. The harmony is straightforward but rich with color.

Michon

Nothing is known about the career of Michon, but the piece dedicated to him by Boüin indicates that he was not unknown among the professional players of his time. His two publications consist of six solo-bass suites and two unaccompanied duos, one of which is for vielle and musette, the only extended composition expressly for this combination. It should be added that this work does not, however, exploit any of the differentiating features of the two instruments. Michon's music is predominantly French, consisting of dance and character pieces; both publications begin with a French overture. In his second publication, Michon follows his opening suite with a "suite en sonate" which contains Adagio-allegro-menuetto-arietta-allegro ma non tropo[!]. The emphasis in this latter work is on the galant style with slow harmonic rhythm and simple harmonies. This feature contrasts with the rich, almost experimental nature of the harmonies of other pieces. For example, the musette which follows the overture in the first suite of the second book is harmonized in a unique way. Because of the drones, most composers would have provided an accompaniment establishing the tonic. Michon uses the relative minor thus creating momentary harmonic ambiguity.

Example 7. Michon, *Amusemens de chambre*, Première suite en divertissement, Musette en rondeau, mm.1-5.

Jean-Baptiste Dupuits

Jean-Baptiste Dupuits was a teacher and composer rather than a well known virtuoso. A student of André Campra, he composed a variety of instrumental and vocal music, revealing a thorough background in composition. The five publications of Jean-Baptiste Dupuits for the vielle represent the pinnacle of the repertory for this instrument both in terms of technical difficulty and musical quality. They comprise two sets of duos, one for melody instrument and vielle and one for two vielles, a set of six solo-bass sonatas preceded and introduced by the method, a set of sonatas for vielle and obbligato harpsichord, and a set of *Pièces de caractère* in the style of the keyboard music of the period. In addition there is a cantata, *Le Bouquet*, for soprano, vielle and bass. With the exception of the latter, all these works were published in 1741, although they must have been composed over a lengthy period. They were published in a particular order which is not based on their chronological order. The first work is the method, discussed elsewhere, the purpose of which is to serve as an introduction to all of the composer's works, since in each one Dupuits refers the player back to the method for further explanation.

The least ambitious and most likely earliest set consists of four duos for vielle and melody instrument in the form of lengthy suites. Clearly the melody instrument of preference for Dupuits is the oboe, a first choice unique in this repertory, although it is frequently mentioned as an alternative. The reason for this choice is one of balance, always a very important consideration of Dupuits since equality of the parts, even accompanimental parts, is a salient feature of his style.[14] Dupuits most likely finds other instruments too soft, although he hedges and lists them as possiblities. In these pieces, as in most duos of this type, the oboe lies mostly below the melody line of the vielle, often providing a bass.

The forty-five *Pièces de caractère* are composed in the style of the harpsichord pieces of the composer's contemporaries. The titles of the pieces can be found in the keyboard works of others, and some bear thematic similarities to other works of this type.[15] The work begins with two suites written for the dedicatee, the maid of honor to the Queen of Spain. These are followed by the pieces in C, concluding with two large works *Le Labyrinthe* and *le Dupuits*. The former represents an extensive movement constructed out of four pieces two rondeaux in duple meter and two menuets in contrasting moods and tonalities which are intermingled. The latter is a four-movement suite which is clearly meant to show off the virtuosity of the player-composer. Both have an experimental quality which in pushing formal and technical boundaries to their limits may not be totally successful. A group of pieces in G follows concluding with one of the composer's longest and finest movements *L'Unique*. This piece is in ritornello form given its concerto features by the nature of the theme and contrasting solos. The unfolding of the form makes this the lengthiest piece in the set. The last solo concludes with a lengthy pedal point which pushes the tonal limits of the instrument (see Example 3).

Not all the pieces in this collection are of equal quality. Occasionally the composer overuses motor rhythms to the point of monotony. While most of the pieces are in binary forms or rondeaux, Dupuits, in works such as *Le Labyrinthe* or *L'Unique*, attempts to transcend them. A mingling of styles creates considerable variety. While *L'Unique* is high baroque, almost German, *La Singulière* is frankly galant. In between are pieces with the rich harmonies and refinement of the rococo.

The set of solo-bass sonatas which accompany the method suffer from the same strengths and weaknesses, as well as mixtures of styles found in

---

[14]See the *Avertissements* in Appendix One.

[15]*Le Petit maître*, for example, is thematically related to the piece of the same name by Jean-François Dandrieu (1682-1738).

the *Pièces de caractère*. Dupuits strives for the utmost contrast in movement order, and each work is totally different in this respect.

Unique in the repertory are the six sonatas for the harpsichord with the
accompaniment of the vielle. They are modelled on the *Pièces de clavecin
en sonates* of Joseph Cassanéa de Mondonville (1711-1722) which appeared
in 1734 and marked the departure from solo-bass textures which had
prevailed in earlier times. Dance movements, fugal movements, and
concerto movements are mingled with arias and other types to create the
greatest possible variety. The interchange, or conversation, between the
instruments is on an equal basis resulting in great textural variety. The
two instruments may take turns accompanying each other or in concerto
movements alternate solos. In fugal movements, the vielle plays one voice
while the right hand and left hand of the harpsichord each take another.
The composer's concern for balance reveals itself in the careful dynamic
markings, shadings which in some cases are almost impossible to create
on the vielle.

The six "sonates" for two vielles are among the most musically and
technically challenging in the repertory. The composer wishes to push the
instrument to its musical limits in the following passage which stretches
the limits of acceptable harmony, given the presence of the drones (G-g-
d').

Example 8. Jean-Baptiste Dupuits, Sonata VI in G Minor for two vielles,
1st mov't, mm.10-18.

In Example 9, the leaps in the second part are extremely difficult to execute cleanly (whether or not the thumb is used). These works, as with many other French sonatas, mingle Italianate movements with character pieces and dance movements associated with the suite.

Example 9. Jean-Baptiste Dupuits, Sonata No.6 in G Minor for two vielles, 2nd mov't., mm.23-32.

Jean-François Boüin

In addition to his method, *La Vielleuse habile*, Boüin published three other musical collections: a set of six suites *Les Muses*, Op.1, before 1742, followed by a set of sonatas Op.2 in 1748, and several sets of variations on popular songs entitled *Les Amusements d'une heure et demie*, Op.4, about 1763.[16] Boüin is at his best when working with melodies, particularly those in a popular vein, or even dance types. It is with disappointment that one finds bass lines of a nature so primitive and at times inept that the composer's background and compositional training might be called into question. These are seldom independent from the upper parts and often move in parallel thirds or sixths with them. Even those works

---

[16]This title is an attempt, perhaps tongue-in-cheek, to top Bâton's earlier work *Les amusements d'une heure.*

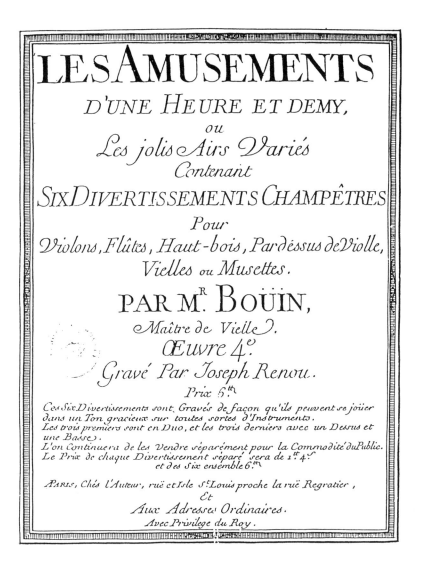

Illustration 4. Jean-François Boüin, *Les Amusements d'une heure et demie*, title page (© cliché Bibliothèque Nationale de France, Paris).

Illustration 5. Ravet, *Suittes et sonates*, Op.1, title page (© cliché Bibliothèque Nationale, Paris).

entitled "fugue" have little counterpoint. As might be expected the works called sonatas are the weakest, as Boüin indulges in the most hackneyed, basic and predictable figuration. Even so, most of these sonatas are made up of dance movements, thus are almost indistinguishable from the suites. Boüin had little feeling for the Italian style.

On the positive side, Boüin clearly knows the capabilities of the instrument and uses the two-octave range with greater freedom than most other composers. Further, many of the individual movements have their charm with or without the bass.

Ravet

Ravet was often classed with Danguy and Bâton as one of the great virtuosi of his time, and his music reflects both for better and for worse this fact. Rapid passage work, often harmonically static, is included for effect and often does not enhance the musical content. Ravet's first work consists primarily of dance movements arranged in suites for two vielles or in solo-bass sonatas. He seems to make little distinction between the two types of pieces. The overuse of parallel movement in thirds and sixths and lack of counterpoint or interplay creates considerable monotony in this work. The Third Suite is, however, a brilliant work which fully exploits the two vielles. Ravet's opus 2 consists of four solo-bass sonatas and three duos for violin and vielle. The four solo-bass works have programmatic titles (*La Militaire, La Marine, La Chasse*, etc.) and movements relating to them. We have fanfares, storms at sea, hunting calls using all the technical and virtuosic tools at the composer's disposal. The bass for these sonatas is unfigured suggesting performance with a sustaining bass instrument minus keyboard. The bass is by no means limited to harmonic support and takes an active role in the proceedings. Fortunately, the duos for vielle and violin are not programmatic and have greater musical interest than the preceding works. The violin and the vielle are treated as equal partners in the texture, and, although the violin is often used in an accompanying role, it is often given extensive passages above the vielle. Ravet does not shrink from exploiting a variety of harmonic possibilities which adds to the variety in these works.

Buterne and Prudent

A number of composers produced only one, or one surviving work for the vielle. This fact does not reflect on the quality of these works, as we shall see. Buterne's surviving opus 2, consisting of four solo-bass sonatas and two duos for two vielles, has been previously recognized for its quality.[17] All sonatas consist of four-five movements beginning with a slow movement, an allegro in the galant style, a pair of contrasting major-minor airs, and a dance movement. Notable is the mixing of major and minor modes. In the third sonata, a major-mode allegro is followed immediately by one in the parallel minor, a technique later used by Boüin. The fourth sonata is notable for its exploitation of the extreme upper range of the instrument. Although there is considerable variety in content, binary form is used almost without exception. The technical and musical demands of the duos are the same as those for the solo-bass works. Their full exploitation of both vielles on an equal basis (although the lower tends to serve most often as accompanist for the upper instrument) makes these works some of the best of their type.

Prudent's collection in contrast is largely unknown.[18] It appears to be a youthful work, as the composer would later gain renown for his vocal works. The publication consists of four solo-bass sonatas and two sonatas for vielle and violin. These sonatas consist of from two to four movements, the first an extensive rondeau or sarabande, the second an allegro which is fugal or has imitative sections, and a dance movement. Thus these works are French interpretations of the church sonata. In contrast to other composers mentioned here, the extensive use of counterpoint in all movements of these works is a unique feature of Prudent's style.[19] Example 10 illustrates the pervasive interest in imitation even in dance movements.

Like Buterne, Prudent is particularly adept at mixing modes. The

---

[17]Eugène de Briqueville, p.78. Buterne's dedication is an enigmatic statement of his philosophy of life. "Music . . . which until the present has amused my leisures today will become my occupation. . . . All men strive for happiness, and I am a bit more of a man than many others. . . . " [La Musique . . . n'a juqu'à présent qu'amusé mes loisirs; elle va faire aujourd'hui mes occupations. . . . Tous les hommes tendent au bonheur; et je suis un peu plus homme que bien d'autres. . . .]

[18]This collection entitled *Les Bouquets de Chassenay* is dedicated to Madame Poncher, Baronne de Chassenay Tours Ste. Parise. From the dedication, a poem in praise of her musical abilities and taste, the implication is that she was a student of Prudent. Each of the sonatas is given a female name, perhaps students of Prudent or members of his patroness's family.

[19]Boüin recognized this. His character piece *Le Prudent* (*Les Muses*, p.18) is imitative throughout, a feature otherwise non-existent in other works of this composer.

second movement of the third sonata *L'Elise* is a fugue which begins in C major but concludes with a surprising restatement of the subject in C minor. Also like Buterne, the fourth sonata *La Monique* pulls out all the stops with extensive use of the upper range of the vielle. Prudent uses a variety of forms, although like his contemporaries he depends heavily on binary form, even in his fugues. The two duos for vielle and violin are disappointing in that the violin serves mostly as an accompanist, remaining in the lower range most of the time.

Example 10.   Prudent, Sonate *L'Elise*, 1st mov't., Sarabande, mm.30-36.

The Methods

Four methods entirely devoted to the vielle were published in eighteenth-century France.[20] In addition, numerous works provide some basic information such as the range and tuning of the instrument in conjunction with a general discussion of instruments. These latter works will be discussed in dealing with specific issues in Chapter 3. A brief discussion of the nature of the methods entirely devoted to the vielle in relation to the repertory is relevant here.

---

[20]Another "method" cited by Edmond van der Straeten, *La Musique aux Pays-Bas*, vol.4 (Brussels: G.-A. Trigt, 1878, Dover rep., 1969): 92 and mentioned by Bröcker,p.327, is in fact a page of notes most likely based on Bouïn's method.

The first method to appear was an anonymous work published by the printer Ballard in 1732 and revised in 1742. It has been suggested that Charles Bâton had some hand in it, and this is certainly possible, since he was at that time the most accomplished player and leader of the trend to make the instrument compatible with chamber music of the period. It was obviously timed to take advantage of the new craze for the instrument, but it has little to offer beyond a brief discussion of the most basic technique and a few pieces. Some of these pieces are most likely by the author of the treatise, but others are arrangements of well-known pieces. There is discussion of a new instrument with the range of two and a half octaves extending down to middle C but retaining the normal tuning of the drones. The author includes at least one piece suited for this instrument, but the experiment was stillborn, and there is no other extant repertory.

The first important method was that of Dupuits, *Principes pour toucher de la viele*, which appeared in 1741. It is important to remember in reading this method that although the instrument itself was old, the techniques to play the music being composed for it were not. There is an experimental quality to the technical ideas presented, and many of these ideas are unique to Dupuits and his music. For example, Dupuits described the use of the thumb in fingering the keyboard, an idea which never caught on, but may be useful in playing the wide-ranging keyboard-like melodies which he composed.[21] In addition, many of the interpretive signs described there are unique to this composer's music. Thus while many concepts represented here are generally applicable, this method is most useful in studying the music of Dupuits himself. Indeed, his discussion of his six sonatas which conclude this method is the most thorough explanation by a composer of his own works to be found in this repertory.

The method of Boüin *La Vielleuse habile*, which appeared in 1761, is arguably one of the most complete methods for any instrument to appear in eighteenth-century France. There are few basic issues which this composer does not discuss, and every point of technique is approached in a systematic and detailed way. The text is illustrated by musical examples, but in addition, the author provides the page numbers of pieces in his other works the suites, op.1 and the sonatas, op.2 which illustrate

---

[21]Although modern methods avoid discussion of this issue, a thorough explanation of using the thumb is found in *Musiques en duo pour vielles à roue*, 2ᵉ recueil. Guy Casteuble, ed. (Courlay: Editions J. M. Fuzeau, 1985): 11-13.

the point.[22] Boüin then provides a progressive set of forty-four lessons from the easiest to the most difficult, explaining what each piece is meant to teach. These are followed by a series of pieces in C and G, which are arrangements of popular songs, and works by Lully, Couperin and others.

Boüin's work owes much to that of Dupuits, and he quotes the latter on a number of occasions (without attribution). These include sections on ornamentation and remarks on aesthetics.[23] Boüin was a practical man, more concerned with the basis of technique, and it may be that the former were issues of little interest to him, nevertheless his approach has its own special charm. A typical example of the mundane advice that Boüin includes can be found in the section dealing with the care of the instrument. Boüin says, "When during humid weather the keys do not fall back in place easily, you should put your vielle in your bed in the morning after you get up, cover it well, and leave it there until the keys fall again easily, ..."[24]

A notable difference between Boüin and Dupuits, however, is the level of the pupil at which their respective methods are aimed. Dupuits assumes a basic musical knowledge and the technical requirements which he lays down are much more advanced than those of Boüin. The sonatas which conclude this method are some of the more difficult works in the literature. Boüin assumes no musical background, and the pieces which he includes for study are of a popular nature with the most basic technical requirements.[25] This observation supports the conclusion that although the instrument had retained, and perhaps even increased, its popularity, it was used in a much more casual way by those who had little interest in the sophisticated literature composed for it in the 1730's, 40's and 50's.

---

[22]It would be useful to have an edition of *La Vielleuse habile* with these pieces from his other works inserted in the text. They often better illustrate his ideas than the examples which are part of the method.

[23]For example compare Dupuit's remarks about the wheel as the soul of the instrument, *Principes*, IV with Boüin, *La Vielleuse habile*, pp.16-17.

[24]Boüin, *La Vielleuse habile*, p.20, "Lorsque dans les tems humides les touches du clavier ne retombent pas aisément, il faut mettre votre Vielle le matin en vous levant dans votre lit, la bien couvrir, & l'y laisser jusqu'à ce que les touches du clavier retombent aisément, ..." The keys fit through slots into the key box, and this fit should be snug but not too tight. In humid weather the keys swell creating this problem.

[25]Claude Flagel, intro., *La Belle vielleuse*, points out that such works were much easier to use for teaching students whose musical literacy was almost non-existent.

The last method to appear in the eighteenth century was that of Michel Corrette, *La Belle vielleuse*, published in 1783. The text of this method is largely a condensation of that of Boüin. The only original part of this work is the paragraph dealing with tuning, an issue surprisingly left untouched by Dupuits and Boüin.[26] The musical examples are similar, in some cases almost identical, to those of Boüin. This method, perversely, was the most popular of its time and was reprinted in the nineteenth century.[27] The music has become a staple of contemporary players of the instrument who venture into the eighteenth-century repertory.[28]

Another anonymous method most certainly intended for publication but never completed survives in manuscript.[29] This method assumes a basic knowledge of music and proceeds directly to a discussion the basic features of technique. However, it devotes more space than any other method to a systematic discussion of fingering. It also includes some comments on ornamentation. It includes a number of airs by Handel, Geminiani and other contemporary composers, some with elaborate variations. While it is impossible to date this method, it was most likely written after 1741 and perhaps much later, since it appears to comment on ideas put forth in Dupuit's method concerning the division of the wheel into more than three and four, and it follows Boüin's general approach in its presentation of the *coup de poignet*.

Bordet's method, passages from which have already been discussed, is not properly speaking a method for the vielle in that it devotes no space to technique, instead referring the student to a method and teacher. Bordet's main interest is the musical skills required for the playing of airs or popular tunes on any instrument. He provides many musical examples

---

[26]Claude Flagel, intro., *La Belle vielleuse*, has compared Corrette's text with that of Dupuits and Boüin and reaches this conclusion. For a discussion of Corrette's remarks on tuning, see Chapter 3.

[27]With certain deletions. See Flagel, intro., *La Belle vielleuse*, on the differences between the original and the nineteenth-century edition.

[28]Claude Flagel has recorded almost all the music found in the method on *La Belle vielleuse*, Editions Pluriel (n.d.). It has been rereleased on compact disc. This recording is important in that it is the first known to me which uses period instruments for this repertory. Other recordings too numerous to mention contain selections from this work.

[29]Paris, Bibliothèque Nationale, Cons. Rés.1177 "Airs choisis pour la viele avec les principes generaux." There are many pages left blank where the author intended to fill in pieces.

arranged as duos, carefully marking each part with its suitability for each instrument with a system of symbols.[30] There are thus duos with such combinations as violin and vielle, musette and vielle, etc.

The music found in all these methods is, with the exception of that of Dupuits, entirely made up of popular airs and dances emphasizing the principal activity of most vielle players.

Music for other Instruments in the Style of the Vielle

There are very few pieces from seventeenth- and eighteenth-century France specifically imitating or evoking the vielle. There are certainly pieces which create drone-like effects, but many of these are called "musette" in imitation of the bagpipe. Others use drones for evoking moods or contexts such as the pastoral without calling to mind a specific instrument. Several for various instruments or ensembles, however, merit some discussion.

The earliest example is the harpsichord piece by François Couperin discussed earlier for its social commentary, "Les Viéleux, et les Gueux," from *Les Fastes de la grande et ancienne Mxnxstrxndxsx*. The left hand is labelled "Bourdon" and imitates the drones with C-G-C broken in such a way to simulate the continuous sound. The upper part is labelled (1er and Second) "air de viéle." The upper part is much like a dance for the vielle played very slowly in a minor key, much in the same way that Camille Saint-Saens satirizes the cancan in the *Carnival of the Animals*. The limping rhythm of the simulated drones creates a musical picture of cripples. The square rhythms of this piece are typical of the style of music often associated with this instrument. In fact, this piece is quite playable on the vielle (an octave up).[31]

Another harpsichord piece of a totally different kind is found in a collection of works by the Parisian organist Pierre Thomas Dufour (c.1721-1786) published in 1772.[32] The piece entitled *La Vielle* eschews any

---

[30]"M" is used for musette, "V" is used for vielle, and a symbol combining the two letters is used for pieces appropriate for both instruments.

[31]In fact, an arrangement is found in J.-B. C. Ballard, *Pièces choisies pour la vielle à l'usage des commençants avec les instructions pour toucher, & pour entretenir cet instrument* (Paris, 1732, 1742): 28-29.

[32]Dufour, *Pièces de clavecin . . .* oeuvre Ier. Paris, 1772: 4. This composer may be related to the M. Dufour listed by Boüin as one of the "habiles gens" (p.13), but at present no definite connection can be made.

programmatic reference to the instrument. It is a gentle, graceful work reflecting some fifty years of respectability for the instrument. The key of A minor is not one associated with music for the vielle. The piece is paired with another entitled "La Musette" with many of the same characteristics.

One of the most interesting evocations of the vielle , however, comes from the greatest French composer of the period, Jean-Philippe Rameau (1683-1764). In *Platée*, a "ballet bouffon", first performed at Versailles in 1745, he introduces "Menuets en goût de vièle" in Act II, scene 5. Here the character "La Folie" demonstrates her musical abilities to move the heart with her lyre. It should be said at the outset that Rameau is not making fun of this character. On the contrary, her musical ability is clearly admired. Throughout the ballet the orchestra imitates all kinds of animals and is challenged to capture all kinds of moods. It is possible that Rameau simply wishes to add to the orchestra's imitative repertory. This bit of program music adds to the topsy-turvy character of this work.

Rameau recreates the sound of the instrument with rhythmically articulated drones in all the strings (D-A). The violins play open D-A strings while playing the melody on the E string. In keeping with the nature of the vielle, woodwinds do not take part.

CHAPTER THREE

MUSICAL INTERPRETATION AND
PERFORMANCE PRACTICE

Some Preliminary Considerations

Eighteenth-century treatises and the scores themselves provide considerable information about how the music was interpreted and about technique, but, as with all sources before the twentieth century, they leave many of the most basic questions unanswered. Eighteenth-century treatises are generally uninterested in the most efficient muscular motion, for example. This seems to be a personal problem to be solved by the player him (or her) self. But perhaps the most basic question is, how did the music actually sound?

There is a large gap in sources between the eighteenth century and the last twenty years, although the playing tradition has been tenuously continuous. As a result, reconstructing the technique of playing the vielle involves stripping away two centuries of accretions while retaining those features of current technique which fill in where the eighteenth-century sources leave off and aid in achieving an interpretation which is musically valid.

Basic Features of the Vielle

The sound of the vielle is created by a wooden wheel which rubs against the strings.[1] The wheel of the vielle functioned like a bow and was exploited with as much flexibility as possible to produce an expressive, singing interpretation of the music. To Boüin, it was the "soul of the

---

[1]The strings should press on the wheel with enough force to produce a clear sound, but they should not change pitch when the wheel is turned quickly. Adjusting the degree of force with which the strings press against the wheel is one way of balancing the drones and the melody strings.

instrument."[2] Since the pressure on the string cannot be varied, as it can on the violin, the only way to achieve expression is to change the speed of the wheel.

In the eighteenth century the wheel was made of one piece of wood (in fact this practice continued into the twentieth century). Because it was lathed across the grain, it was never perfectly round, and the grain on each side of the wheel went in a different direction.[3] With a wheel of this construction, the rosin tends to redistribute itself, resulting in a slight wavering in the sound in the highest notes. Composers avoided exposing this flaw by including these notes only in fast pieces, where the speed of the wheel minimized the effect, or by passing over them quickly.

The vielle has six strings. Two are melody strings which run through the key box on top of the instrument and are tuned in unison g'. The main reason for having two melody strings is to establish the dominance of the melody over the drones. Tangents attached to sliding keys simultaneously stop both these strings. These keys are pressed against the strings by the player and then fall back in place from gravity, since the instrument is slightly tilted away from the player. These keys fit through slots cut in the side of the key box, and must not fit too tightly in order to avoid sticking, but still must be loose enough to move freely. In the early 1730's, keys were added to give the instrument a range of two chromatic octaves (with the exception of the highest F natural-F sharp key which must be tuned to either one or the other, depending on its use in the piece).

Four drone strings run along the sides of the keybox. Depending on the tuning, only three are used at any one time. Thus in C (major or minor), the drones tuned c-g-c' are used, while in G (major or minor) G-g-d' are used. In other words, in tuning from C to G, the lowest c, or bourdon, is disconnected and the G added, while the c' is tuned up to d', either by tightening the string or using a tuning device which shortens its length (see Illustration 6) called a "drapeau (flag)", or sometimes today, a capo. The latter string, known as the trompette, runs across a movable bridge which vibrates against the top of the instrument when the speed

---

[2]Bouïn, *La Vielleuse habile*, p.16.

[3]Nowadays most makers band the wheel with a strip of wood so that the grain goes in one direction. The wheel can then be made perfectly round. This means of construction was certainly possible for eighteenth-century makers, but they probably did not regard this as an important problem.

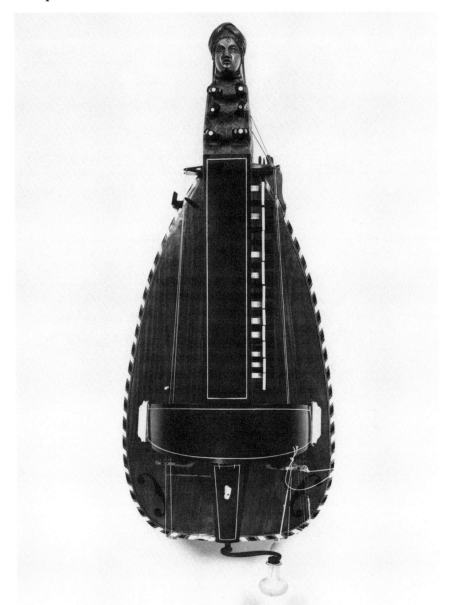

Illustration 6. *Vielle en luth* by François Feury, c.1740 (note "drapeau" at upper left side of body).

Illustration 7. Wheel with *trompette*.

of the wheel is suddenly increased.[4] On larger instruments four sympathetic strings run along the body and are most often tuned in unison with the melody strings, although some alternative tunings are possible.[5]

Example 1.   Tuning and range of the vielle as found in Diderot's *Encyclopédie.*

As discussed in the last chapter, Henri Bâton perfected the vielle by building the instrument on the backs of old guitars and lutes. While few instruments verifiably constructed in this way survive, most instruments were constructed in the eighteenth century using bodies with these shapes. Boüin tells us that the lute-shaped instrument (*vielle en luth*) is appropriate for large concert halls and the guitar-shaped instrument (*vielle en guitarre*) is appropriate for chamber music.[6] Two levels of sound then result from these two different instruments.[7] Musicians differed as to which of these two types they preferred. Boüin favors the larger instrument, because it produces more *harmonie,* which may be translated as resonance. Dupuits

---

[4]In the nineteenth century, this moveable bridge became known as a "chien," literally translated as "dog," because it is shaped like one. Constructing one to respond easily on a particular instrument is one of the most difficult problems for any player. None to my knowledge has survived from the eighteenth century.

[5]Boüin, p.15, discusses the tuning of as many as six sympathetic strings tuned in the tonic triad. The problem with this arrangement is that the player often plays alternatively in C and G, and retuning the sympathetic strings for each change of tuning would be cumbersome.

[6]Boüin, p.20.

[7]See the *Avertissement* of Dupuits' *Sonates pour un clavecin et une viele* for further discussion of this point.

favors smaller instruments, because they balance better with the harpsichord and other instruments in chamber music. In part this difference in
opinion is the result of a difference in their respective musical styles and
types of musical activity. Boüin had in mind the musical activity of most
amateurs, which was the performance of popular airs, either as solos or
as unaccompanied duos. In Boüin's music, there is likely to be no balance
problem, since in solo-bass works, the vielle always dominates and
accompaniments remain just that, whereas in the music of Dupuits the
basses are of equal importance with the melody. It is well to remember
the experimental nature of the construction of these instruments. After the
initial phase of development, makers often built larger guitar-shaped
instruments and smaller lute-shaped instruments, although the distinction
between the two remained. There was simply no standardization in size.

The requirements of the music demand an instrument which speaks
extremely quickly and clearly in order to execute the *agréments* which are
as prevalent in this music, as they are in any French music of the period.
In fact, based on the experience of this author, instruments made in the
eighteenth century and restored to playable condition do have this
characteristic.

Tuning

The vielle possesses a melodic range of two chromatic octaves from g'
to g'''. The tangents which control the pitch of the individual notes can
be tuned precisely, and the preset pitch cannot be altered in any way in
performance. The keyboard of the vielle is thus analogous to that of any
other keyboard instrument, and therefore, questions of temperament are
relevant.[8] Michel Corrette is alone in his discussion of this subject.
Perhaps Corrette's background as a keyboard player made him more
sensitive to this issue. Corrette's description for tuning the melody strings
of the vielle is very short and is ambiguous on a number of points.
However, it has been possible to piece together enough information to
make Corrette's directions useable.

The string named the trumpet is tuned in Ut and the two strings in the

---

[8]Tuning questions are particularly important when a harpsichord is part of the
ensemble, since the uncompromising nature of the vielle highlights any clashes in
intonation.

keybox are tuned to the unison of Sol (B) [so that] the fifth [is] a bit narrow against the Ut (A); [as are] also the fifths C, D, E, F and G, H, I a little less [narrow] and with regard to the other fifths a bit stronger; one must take care to disengage the trumpet after the fifth Sol and the octaves of Ut are tuned." [9]

More simply, tune the trumpet to C. Then tune the melody strings to G in unison, using a narrow fifth between the trumpet and the melody strings. Then tune the octave C with the trumpet. Disengage the trumpet and tune the other C. The fifths C-G, G-D, D-A, and A-E are all the same size. The fifths E-B, B-F sharp, and F sharp-C sharp are a little less narrow. The fifths C-F, F-B flat, B flat-E flat, E flat-A flat are stronger, or even less tempered than the previous fifths.

There are thus three sizes of fifths, and, therefore, this is not equal temperament.[10] The description is very close that of the *tempérament ordinaire* of Jean-Le Rond D'Alembert (1717-1783) in his theoretical work *Eléments de musique théorique et pratique suivant les principes de M. Rameau* (1752), p.48, except that Corrette has left out explanatory material which would have reduced the ambiguity.[11]   It is possible to interpret

[9]Corrette, *La belle vielleuse*, p.1, "On accorde dabord [!] la corde nomée trompette en Ut A ensuite les 2 cordes dans le Clavier à l'unisson du Sol B et la quinte un peu foible sur l'ut A; ainsi que les quintes C.D.E.F. et celles G.H.I. un peu moins, et a [!] l'egard des autres quintes k, l, m, n, un peu plus fortes; il faut avoir soin d'accrocher la trompette, après que la 5te sol B. et les octaves d'ut sont accordées.

[10]I wish to thank Professor Owen Jorgensen for his assistance in interpreting the Corrette passage; the conclusions which follow are the result of our correspondence.

[11]For a translation and discussion of D'Alembert's description, see Owen Jorgensen, *Tuning* (East Lansing: Michigan State University Press, 1991): 193.

D'Alembert and thus Corrette in two ways. A rigidly theoretical approach would result in a system favoring heavily the sharp keys and would create especially harsh effects in C minor, one of the most heavily used sonorities on the vielle, since the interval E-flat-G is a wolf tone.[12]   A freer interpretation of D'Alembert (and Corrette), however, provides a compromise especially conducive to the music for the vielle in that the intervals in C major-C minor and G major-G minor are favored.[13]   Of particular use is Corrette's description would have been a discussion of the quality of the thirds which result from his method of tuning. Without them, this description will always be subject to some interpretation.

Corrette is the only author to mention the need to tune the drones a little narrow. With a tempered tuning the fifths of the keyboard are wide, and if the drones are tuned in perfect fifths, they will be out of tune with the keyboard.

Dynamics

The vielle is capable of playing both loud (*fort*) and soft (*doux*), and these "terrace dynamics" are often found in the music. The difference between these two levels of sound is achieved by the contrast between articulated playing (created by the *coup de poignet* described below) and playing with a smooth turning of the wheel named by Boüin *en musette* for its resemblance to the sound of that instrument.[14]   When playing *en musette*, limited gradations and swells (*enflés*) are possible, resulting in an expressive, singing style.[15]

Some movements are played entirely *en musette*. Boüin characterizes them in the following way, "In tender airs, or musettes, there is no prescribed *coup de poignet*. One can turn the wheel more or less quickly

---

[12]*Ibid.* 193-202.

[13]*Ibid.* 203-213.

[14]Boüin, p.17.

[15]Dupuits, VIII, gives three signs for changing the speed of the wheel; a horizontal line for turning the wheel faster but steadily, an asterisk for increasing the speed gradually (enflé), and a u-shaped mark for crescendo-diminuendo. However, these marks are rarely found, even in the music of Dupuits himself.

according to the character of the airs. . . ." [16]   The suites of Michon often
contain paired dance movements, where the second dance is marked
"doux," indicating that it should be played without *coup de poignet*. This
practice was standard even where it was not indicated. The Ballard
method says, ". . . it should be observed that ordinarily, when two
menuets are played, and one is in major and the other minor, the first
which is in major is played detaching all the notes with the *poignet*, and
the other, which is in minor, is played *en musette*, that is to say softly
turning always equally." [17]

Most often, directions for dynamics in the music reveal, as one might
expect, the introduction of contrast between sections or phrases. They also
reveal the necessity of creating balance within the ensemble, such as when
the vielle must move into the background and other parts must come to
the fore.   Dupuits summarizes the possibilities of using this type of
contrast within a piece:

1. Where the melody is repeated.

2. Where the melody is less active (i.e., more lyrical).

3. Where the bass has an active part.

4. Near (just before) a passage which one wishes to make standout.[18]

---

[16]Boüin, p.17, "Dans les airs tendres, ou Musettes, il n'y a point de coup de poignet
déterminé. On peut tourner la roüe plus ou moins vite, selon le caractere des airs; . . ."

[17]Anon., *Pièces choisies pour la vièle à l'usage des commençants; avec des instructions pour
toucher, & pour entretenir cet instrument* (Paris: J.-B.-Christophe Ballard, 1741), p.12, ". . . il
faut observer qu'ordinairement, lorsque l'on joüe deux Menuets, dont l'un est majeur &
l'autre mineur, le premier qui est majeur se joüe, en détachant toutes les notes du poignet,
& l'autre qui est mineur se joüe en musette, c'est-à-dire doucement & en tournant toûjours
également."

[18]Dupuits VIII, "Dans les pièces de mouvement, quoi qu'il semble que tout doit être
marqué, cela n'empêche pas qu'on ne puisse passer plusieurs mesures sans les détacher,
sur tout lorsqu'il y a des répétitions de chants, ou que le chant travaille moins, ou pendant
que la Basse aura quelques traits d'exécutions, ou lorsqu'on est prés d'un passage qu'on
veut faire paroître, parce-qu'il faut que chaque partie d'une pièce contribue à se faire
distinguer l'un de l'autre, pour rendre la pièce interessante. Fig.56."

He provides the following musical example (Fig.56):

The *Coup de poignet*

The most characteristic feature of the sound of the vielle is the vibrating bridge which supports the drone string which is known as the *trompette*. The term *coup de poignet* has mystified modern players, because "wrist stroke" does not seem to describe what happens, in fact quite the opposite. The *coup de poignet*, however, is the basic bow stroke associated with the bass viol and described in detail by Etienne Loulié in his manuscript treatise on that instrument.[19] In this stroke, as it is used on the bass viol, the middle finger of the left hand leans heavily on the stick of the bow as if to scratch the string. As soon as the sound begins, the tension is released. The sharp articulation followed by a sustained sound which results in a plucking effect is analogous to the sound created by the vielle. This sharply articulated effect was described by various writers at the beginning of the eighteenth century as the basic *French* bow stroke for

---

[19]Etienne Loulié, "Méthode pour apprendre à jouer la viole" (Paris, Bibliothèque Nationale, Ms. fonds fr.n.a.6355), fol.218ᵛ. These passages have been much discussed in secondary literature. See John Hsu, *A Handbook of French Baroque Viol Technique* (New York: Broude Brothers Limited, 1981): 2-9.

the violin, as well as the viol, in comparison to the sustained sound which characterized the *Italian* bow stroke.   As the Italian style became more prominent in France towards the middle of the century, this basic bow stroke in violin playing was discarded, and this change in attitude is reflected in later discussions of the *coup de poignet* on the vielle. Charles Bâton published a *Memoire sur la vielle en D-la-re* in the *Mercure de France* of October, 1752. In this work, he attacks the *coup de poignet* as being too harsh. Instead, he feels that the touch alone of the fingers of the left hand is sufficient to achieve an articulation approximating that of the flute or violin. The *coup de poignet* may have had much to do with the loss in popularity of the vielle as an appropriate instrument for sophisticated chamber music after 1760.

All writers discuss the use of the *coup de poignet* to bring out the character of the music and to create as much variety as possible.   In describing the use of the *coup de poignet* in the chaconne, for example, the anonymous manuscript method says, "It is necessary to attempt in this movement [the chaconne] the *coup de roue* as much as possible, that is to say detach, to slur, to articulate according to the different characters of phrases of which it is made up." [20] Thus the *coup de poignet* was only one means of expression for the vielle.

Continuo Instruments

While the harpsichord was no doubt used heavily in chamber music with the vielle, the combination of these two instruments poses certain problems of balance.   The articulation of the vielle followed by its sustained sound can cover the harpsichord. Dupuits and others seek to overcome this problem through the use of dynamics (see above).[21] Also, the size of the vielle has much to do with this. In his *Sonates*, Dupuits prefers the smaller guitar-shaped instrument.

Some pieces are composed in a way that a bass instrument without harpsichord suffices for the accompaniment. Dupuits' preface to his *Pièces*

---

[20]Paris, Bibliothèque Nationale, Ms. Cons. Rés. 1177 "Airs choisis pour la viele avec les principes generaux,"f.7ᵛ, "Il faut tacher dans ce mouvement de varier le coup de roue autant qu'il est possible, c'est a dire de le detacher, couler, ou piquer suivant les differents caracteres des frases qui le composent."

[21]See Dupuits' *Avertissement* to the *Sonates*, Appendix One for extensive discussion of this point.

de caractère states that these pieces are best performed with the bass alone, although figures are provided. His reasons for this are, ". . . some spot is always found where a delicate ear is not entirely satisfied" with the exactitude of the figures. My interpretation of this passage is that the full realization of the harmonies interacting with the drones create dissonances which might disturb some listeners. Dupuits alludes to the two-part nature of these pieces when he says, ". . . it is very important that the accompanimental part (which is the bassline) be executed with as much attention as if it were the principal part."

While there are a few works specifically for vielle and bass without harpsichord, there are many others which are as effective, if not more so, when they are performed in this way.[22] The vielle has an advantage over other instruments in that it provides its own pseudo-filler. The two-part nature of the texture is the best test of the effectiveness of this method of performance. In any case, the music for vielle and continuo *always* benefits from a sustaining bass instrument given the sustained sound of the upper part and the presence of the drones.

Rhythmic Inequality

The literature on inequality in French music is extensive, and the intention here is to explore it only as it relates to the unique features of the vielle.[23] On the vielle, unequal pairs of notes can be articulated in several ways:

---

[22]Considerable evidence suggests that solo-bass pieces for all instruments were frequently performed without the harpsichord and with only a sustaining bass instrument at least in social situations involving amateurs in eighteenth-century France. Hubert Le Blanc, *Défense de la basse de viole contre les enterprises du violon et les prétensions du violoncel* (Amsterdam, 1740), for example, says, "There is more unity in character required for sweetness in the affairs of life; the evenness of the Viol is more suitable for a gentleman's use, for he finds there an amiable link with society, be it that a Lady sings, plays the Pardessus de Viole, or plays the bass on the harpsichord." trans. by Barbara Garvey Jackson, *Journal of the Viola da Gamba Society of America* 11 (1974): 25. The emphasis here is on the interaction of two people, one the accompanist on the harpsichord or bass viol, the other the soloist. A third would be an intrusion given the social nature of this musical activity. The scores themselves are large enough to be read by only two people, whatever the combination of instruments.

[23]The most recent and thorough survey of this subject is Stephen E. Hefling, *Rhythmic Alteration in Seventeenth- and Eighteenth-Century Music* (New York: Schirmer Books, 1993).

1.   They can be articulated solely with the fingers of the left hand.

2.   The first note of each pair can be articulated with the *coup de poignet* and the second solely with the left hand. In other words, the coup de poignet marks the accented note.

3.   Both notes of a pair can be articulated with the *coup de poignet* in an unequal fashion.

The first two are invariably used when slurs (but not dots or accents) are present. Boüin uses the term "coulé" to describe this usage. The third case is used in highly articulated movements, such as marches and overtures. Boüin uses the term "marqué" to refer to these situations.[24] The diagrams which illustrate the coup de poignet appear to the casual reader to be rhythmically rigid. If a note is shortened or lengthened, however, the distance the wheel travels remains the same, but the <u>speed</u> of the wheel changes providing more possibility for rhythmic subtlety than might first appear.

For example, Boüin's figure 118 (see diagram) shows a wheel divided into four equal quarters, but Boüin marks each quarter "long" or "breve". In other words, the player would turn the wheel more slowly for the first quarter turn and faster for the second, and so on. A close look at the diagrams for the division of the wheel by Boüin indicates that inequality, both with and without the *coup de poignet*, was a fundamental feature of his style, and he probably used it in situations where many or most composers would have avoided it.

The most extensive and systematic discussion of inequality as it applies to the literature for the vielle is found in Boüin's treatise. With a discussion of each meter (pages 6-11), he explains which note values within the meter are unequal. With each meter, he provides a list of

---

[24]Boüin uses the word "marqué" to refer to articulation of the rhythm with the *coup de poignet*. On page 17, he says "Dans les airs gais & vifs, il faut marquer les tours de la roüe avec le poignet. On peut aussi quelquefois ne les pas marquer, cela dépend & du caractere de la Piece & du goût du Joueur (In gay and quick airs, it is necessary to articulate the rotations of the wheel with the coup de poignet. On may sometimes avoid articulating them, but that depends on the character of the piece and the taste of the player)." Helfling 22-23, seems to equate Boüin's use of the term with inequality itself when it in fact refers merely to the articulation of the rhythm. Dupuits also uses "marquer" in the same way. Dupuits and others also use "détaché" to refer to the articulation of the individual notes with the *coup de poignet*. The two terms are almost synonymous.

pieces in his two books of suites and sonatas (see bibliography) which illustrate his observations. While he does not specify clearly which of the pieces he cites are played unequally, it is reasonably easy to determine this based on principals articulated in most eighteenth-century treatises. As a result, it is possible to say that fully half, and perhaps many more, of his examples are to be played unequally, a larger percentage than found in the music for the vielle or any other instrument of this period (c.1750). There may have been much less unanimity concerning the use of inequality in the mid-eighteenth century than is generally supposed. While occasionally ambiguous about which pieces would be normally played with inequality, he is occasionally dogmatic about the types of pieces would always be played unequally, or those which would be always played equally.

Boüin's Figure 118 from *La Belle vielleuse* p.29, showing the divisions of the wheel for the *coup de quatre*, or division of the wheel in four. Note that the first quarter is marked "long" and the second "breve," indicating that the second should be played in a shorter time than the first, although the wheel travels the same distance.

No Unequal values

1. Airs in 2 or C which are "gai or "léger" and contain no sixteenths.

2. Tambourins.

Always Unequal

1. "Airs d'un caractère grave et picqués," such as marches and overtures. The eighths are played "inégales et marquées."[25]

2. In airs in "3" with a slow tempo, the eighths are always played "inégales et coulées."

3. In airs labelled "tendre et gracieux," with many sixteenths, the latter are always played unequally.

4. If one wishes to play a gigue in 6/8 "picqué," a group of three eighth notes may be altered by dotting the first and making the second a sixteenth.

Dupuits in contrast never discusses inequality in any systematic way, although he implies its use by specifying certain movements in his sonatas to be played equally.[26] In part, Dupuit's silence may be a matter of style: he tended to compose in a way which seldom calls for it.

Ornamentation

Ornamentation in French music of this period is too well documented to require exhaustive treatment here. What follows is a discussion of ornamentation as it specifically relates to the performance of music on the vielle. The first composer to publish music specifically for the vielle, Charles Bâton, used only three ornament signs in his publications. Although he never discussed exactly what these signs meant to him, it is relatively easy to imagine how they were played from their usage and from the other composers who did discuss them. They are:

+   a trill beginning on the upper auxiliary.

v   port de voix.

---

[25]Boüin uses the term "picqué" to refer to dotted, or strongly dotted rhythms.

[26]Dupuits X-XI.

⌣ a short trill beginning on the main note.

Rés.1177 discusses these three ornaments in concise and explicit terms and adds the *pincé*, explaining it as analogous to its use on the harpsichord.[27]

Dupuits includes a detailed and precise description of ornaments and their execution as part of his method.[28] Although Dupuits retains the signs established by Bâton as standard for the music for the vielle, Dupuits adds a further selection of signs derived from the harpsichord tradition, most likely the result of the composer's background in this instrument.

Boüin discusses ornaments in two places in his treatise.[29] The first discussion centers around the three ornaments most commonly used. He calls the short trill *martellement*, a confusing term in that it is sometimes used synonymously with *pincé*. Most unusual in Boüin's discussion is his definition of the *coulé* as a *port de voix* in a descending passage and to be played expressively, in other words, an ornament played on the beat, an appoggiatura from above. He provides examples which reenforce this interpretation. Later he discusses the *coulé* as the filling in of a third and gives different examples from his previous discussion which are clearly off-beat ornaments. The repetitions and inconsistencies in his two different discussions of ornaments may be partially explained in that the second is a summary of the discussion found in Dupuits.

Special Techniques

Double stopping was a technique developed for the musette and involved playing two notes simultaneously on the two chanters. Although the pitches played in this way were limited by the respective ranges of the chanters it is quite possible to play contrapuntal passages. Double stopping on the vielle was in fact a fast trill. Boüin describes it in the following way: "... Play and hold the lowest note with one finger and trill

---

[27]Paris, Bibliothèque Nationale, Ms. Cons. Rés.1177, f.12^{r-v}.

[28]Dupuits, p.III, *Des Cadences*.

[29]Boüin, p.4, Article IV Des signes d'agrémens; pp.18-19 *Des agrémens, De la cadence*.

the highest note during the value of the lowest." [30]   Extensive passages of two-part writing are found in the more virtuosic works of the Chédevilles.   While quite difficult technically, these passages are more readily realizable on the musette than on the vielle.

Doubling the turns of the wheel, or, in other words, turning the wheel twice as fast, in order to create a continuous buzz, is a technique commonly used in folk music today for expressive purposes, but in the eighteenth century it was used and only very sparingly in slow, grave pieces, such as marches and overtures.   Boüin discusses briefly the doubling of wheel turns but does not specifically mention the effect. [31]

Disconnecting the drones and playing only with one melody string is a technique which appears to have originated in folk music and is often been used in the performance of the eighteenth-century repertory today. In fact, there is no evidence that any piece was played in the eighteenth century without the drones.   The sole discussion of this occurs in Bordet's method as a last resort for playing those pieces which one wishes to arrange for the vielle but which modulate into "unbearable" keys. Disconnecting the drones " . . . in truth would change the nature of the instruments [musette and vielle] and would take away the greater part of their appeal." [32]

---

[30]Boüin, p.20, ". . . il faut toucher & tenir la note la plus basse avec un doigt, & cadencer pendant la valeur de la note d'en bas, la note la plus haute."

[31]Boüin, p.6-7, discusses its use and marks the notes in which it is used with an asterisk (fig.63, "Marche des mousquetaires"). However, surprisingly, there are other expressive pieces where an asterisk is present, such as the fig.122, the "Musette de M^r. Gaviniés" and several.

[32]Bordet, *Méthode*, p.13, ". . . ce qui à la vérité changeroit la nature de ces instruments, & leur oteroit la plus grande partie de leur agrément."

CHAPTER 4

THE REPERTORY

The following is a list of publications and manuscripts which mention the vielle as an instrument which may be used to play the music contained therein. As has been shown elsewhere, the list of alternate instruments on title pages of eighteenth-century French publications are not haphazard. On the contrary, they are arranged in a hierarchical order, the most suitable instruments being listed first. This principle is particularly important in examining the works for vielle, as almost always, the musette is listed as a suitable instrument as well. The most suitable of the two instruments is generally listed first: a work designated as for "vielle and musette" is primarily suited to the former, but a work designated for "musette and vielle" is intended primarily for the musette. This distinction is very real, since the two instruments have different ranges and different capabilities, thus a set of suites for "musette or vielle" may contain several pieces which contain low F sharps, below the range of the vielle. Likewise, a set of pieces for "vielle or musette" may contain several which go above the range of the latter instrument and articulation markings and dynamics which are impossible on the musette. Frequently in these latter works, the composer has included transpositions for the musette for those places which use the full two-octave range of the vielle. Nevertheless various circumstances have resulted in the absence of the vielle from a title page. For example, the works of Hotteterre for musettes were published before the vielle was a viable alternative. Their appeal, however, has made them a staple of the vielle repertory. The absence of the vielle from collections of arrangements of airs and dances is less clear, but in these cases the title pages have been the deciding factor.

The modern editions included here are of necessity highly selective. Their inclusion is based on their quality. Preference is given to those editions which reproduce the complete publication over those which may contain a single selection from that work. A number of facsimile editions of this music were produced by UCP (Paris) and Early Music Facsimiles (Ypsilanti). Although these companies no longer exist, these editions are often available in large libraries.

I Publications

Anet, Jean-Baptiste (1661-1755). *Deuxième oeuvre de Mr Baptiste, contenant deux suittes de pièces à deux musettes qui conviennent à la flûte traversière, haubois, violons, comme aussi aux vielles.* Paris, 1726.

Terrasson, *Dissertation*, p.98, mentions this as one of the first works for the vielle. It consists of two suites, one in C and one in G. It was later republished in 1730 as *Premier oeuvre de musettes. . . corrigé et augmenté par Mr. Baptiste.* In this latter edition, each suite has an additional piece. The *Deuxième oeuvre* is not to be confused with the *Second oeuvre de musettes* (1730) which contains a different set of suites. For a reason not immediately clear, the vielle is not mentioned on the title page of this latter work.

___. *3e oeuvre de musettes pour le violon, flûte traversière et vielles.* Paris [1734]. Consists of two suites of dance movements and character pieces, one in C and one in G. Modern edition: Sonata I° [for 2 flutes and bc.], Siècle musicale.

Anon. *Amusement champêtre ou les aventures de Cythère. Chansons nouvelle à danser lesquelles se jouent sur la flûte, vielle, musette, &c.*
A collection of unaccompanied airs divided into two parts. This collection is part of a larger series which mentions the musette but not the vielle on most of its title pages.

Anon. *Le Père Barnaba. Vaudeville pour la musette ou viele, avec les veritables paroles.* Paris [n.d.].

Anon. *Ier Recueil de pièces françoises et italiennes, petits airs, romances, vaudevilles . . . choisis dans les opéra comiques du Bucheron, le Roy, et son Fermier, On s'avise jamais de tout, le Maréchal, le Cadi, Anette et Lubin accomodés pour deux vielles ou musettes.* [c.1765]
Pieces arranged for two vielles from the comic operas of Blaise, Duni, Monsigny and Philidor.

Anon. *Suitte de vaudevilles. Recueil de pièces choisies et ajustées pour la musette avec la basse continue qui convienent aux vielle, fluttes à bec, &c.* Paris [n.d.].

Aubert, Jacques (1689-1753). *Concert de simphonies pour les muzettes, vielles, violons, flûtes, et hautbois . . . VI suite.* Paris [1733].
Aubert composed 11 suites for two melody instruments and bass. Only this one, Suite VI, call for musettes and vielles. The others are for violin, flute, or oboe.

___. *Les amuzettes, pièces pour les vièles, musettes, violons, flûtes et hautbois. Oeuvre XIVᵉ.* Paris [1734].
Six solo-bass suites of character pieces. Facsimile edition: Early Music Facsimiles (EMF #2).

___. *Les petits concerts. Duos pour les musettes, vielles, violons, flûtes et hautbois. Oeuvre 16e.* Paris [1734].
Six suites of character pieces for two instruments. Modern edition: Heinrichshofen, 2 vols., N1387, N1388.

Ballard, Jean-Baptiste Christophe (c.1663-1750). See methods.

Bâton, Charles (early 18th c.-after 1754). *Premier oeuvre contenant trois suites pour deux vielles, muzettes, flûtes traversières, flûtes à bec, et hautbois avec la basse continue.* Paris, 1733.
The first three suites are for two instruments unaccompanied and are followed by three solo-bass suites (six suites in all). Facsimile edition: Early Music Facsimiles (EMF #5).

___. *Receuil de pièces à deux musettes qui conviennent aux vielles et autres instruments.* Paris, 1733.

___. *La vielle amusante. Divertissement en six suites pour les vielles, musettes, flûtes traversières, flûtes à bec, et hautbois avec la basse continue. Oeuvre 2e.* Paris [c.1734].
Modern edition: Iᵉʳ Suite [recorder & bc], Schott 10975.

___. *Six sonates pour la vielle... oeuvre IIIe.* Paris [1741].
Four solo-bass sonatas followed by two sonatas for two vielles unaccompanied. Certain movements contain useful articulation markings. Although these works are called sonatas, they are primarily French in character. They contain many virtuosic elements idiomatically appropriate to the instrument. Published together in a facsimile edition with *Les amusements d'une heure, oeuvre IVᵉ* by Éditions Minkoff.

___. *Les amusements d'une heure, duos pour la vièle et la muzette. Oeuvre IVᵉ.* Paris [1748].
Two extended suites or "Amusements" for two unaccompanied instruments. Published together in a facsimile edition with the *Six*

sonates, oeuvre III by Éditions Minkoff.

Bertin, Servais. *Airs sérieux et à boire à une et à deux voix, air pour la vielle et la musette et vaudevilles. . . premier oeuvre.* Paris, 1736.

Boismortier, Joseph Bodin de (1689-1755). *Unzième oeuvre. . . contenant VI suites de pièces à deux muzettes, qui conviennent aux vielles, flûtes-à-bec, traversières & hautbois.* Paris, 1726.
Six suites of dances and character pieces for two instruments.
Modern edition: Leichte Duos, Heinrichshofen, 2 vols. N1302, N1303.
___. *XVIIe Oeuvre. . . contenant VI suites à deux musettes, qui conviennent aux vièles, flûtes-à-bec, traversières, & hautbois.* Paris, 1727.
Six suites of character pieces and dances. Modern edition: 6 Easy Duets, Hortus Musicus 206.
___. *Vingt-et-un^{ème} oeuvre . . . contenant six concerto pour les flûtes-traversières, violons, ou haubois, avec la basse, on peut les jouer en trio en obmettant le ripieno, le dessus du 3e se joue sur la muzette ou sur la flûte-à-bec.* Paris, 1728.
Although this work mentions only musette, it is quite effective on the vielle as well. Modern edition: Concerto Op.21, no.3 [arr. as a trio], Schott 125.
___. *Vingt septième oeuvre, contenant six suites pour deux vièles, musettes, flûtes-à-bec, flûtes traversières et haubois. Suivies de deux sonates à dessus et basse.* Paris, 1730.
Six suites of character pieces and dances in duo followed by two solo-bass sonatas. The latter works mingle Italian and French movements.
Modern edition: Sechs kleine Suiten, Hortus Musicus 206.
Zwei Sonaten, Edition Schott 5738.
___. *Vingt huitième oeuvre. . . contenant 6 sonates en trio pour deux hautbois, flûtes traversières ou violons, avec la basse, suivies de deux concerts, dont le premier se joue sur la musette, la vièle ou la flûte à bec.* Paris [1730].
Modern edition: Konzert C-dur "Zampogna" (Op.28, no.7). Baden: Deutscher Ricordi Verlag.
___. *Trente-troisième oeuvre de Mr. Boismortier contenant six gentillesses en trois parties pour la musette, la vièle et la basse; qui peuvent se jouer aussi sur la flûte à bec, flûte traversière, haubois, ou violon.* Paris, 1731.
The gentilesses are concerto-like trios generally in three movements (F-S-F) which mingle French dances with Italianate features. The use of unison, particularly in the ritornellos make them most suitable for

drone instruments.

__. *Oeuvre quarante-deuxième. . . six pastorales pour deux musettes, ou vièles, qui conviennent aux flûtes-à-bec, flûtes-traversières et haubois.* Paris, 1732. Modern edition: Zes pastorales voor twee melodie-instrumenten. Amsterdam: Muziekuitgeverij Ixyzet.

__. *Second livre de gentillesses en trois parties, pour les musettes, vièles, haubois, violons, flûtes-à-bec, ou traversières, avec la basse, oeuvre 45.* Paris, 1733.

__. *Oeuvre quarante neuvième. . . contenant II divertissements de campagne pour une musette ou vièle seule avec la basse qui conviennent aux flûtes à bec, flûtes traversières, violons, ou haubois.* Paris, 1734. Two extended suites of dances. Although for the most part playable on the vielle, they are intended primarily for the musette. Extensive passages in double stops found in some pieces is not possible on the latter instrument. Modern edition: Divertissement de campagne No.2, Heinrichshofen N3489.

__. *IV balets de village en trio, pour les musettes, vièles, flûtes-à-bec, violons, haubois, ou flûtes traversières, oeuvre 52.* Paris, 1734. Six continuous movements made up of short contrasting sections for two melody instruments and continuo. Modern edition: Ballet de Village en trio, Op.52, no.4; Heinrichshofen N2012.

__. *Noëls en concerto à 4 parties pour les musettes, vièles, violons, flûtes, et haubois. . . oeuvre 68e.* Paris, 1737. This work cannot be reconstructed, since only one part survives.

__. *Oeuvre soixante neuvième. . . fragments melodiques ou symphonies en trois parties mêlées de trio pour les musettes, vièles, flûtes et violons avec la basse. Livre IIe.* Paris, 1737. A large suite of of dances airs champêtre, etc. for two melody instruments and continuo.

__. *Oeuvre soixante-et-douzième. . . contenant six sonates pour la vièle ou musette avec la basse, de toutes les notes qui se trouveront les unes sur les autres, celles d'en bas serviront pour la musette.* Paris [1738]. Six technically difficult sonatas which use the full capabilities of the vielle. Upper register parts are transposed down for alternate performance on the musette.

__. *Nouvelles gentilesses pour une musette et un violon ou haubois avec la basse . . . oeuvre centième.* Paris [c.1741]. Unlike the earlier gentilesses which are most appropriate for two musettes or vièles, these contrast the drone instrument with the violin.

Works without Opus Numbers

___. *Hilas. Cantatille, à voix seule, accompagnée d'une musette ou viele avec la basse.* Paris, 1738.
This short work is primarily intended for the musette.
___. *Les loisirs de bercail, ou simphonies pour une musette ou vièle et un violon sans basse.* Paris [c.1741].
Six unaccompanied suites which contrast the drone instrument with the violin.

Bordet, Toussaint. See Methods and Collections.
___. *Second livre ou recueil d'airs en duo. Choisis et ajustés pour les flûtes, violons, et pardessus de viole dont la plus part peuvent se jouer ur la vielle et la musette. . . divisés en sept suittes avec un prélude sur chaque ton.* Paris, 1755.
As with the method and first book, Bordet indicates the appropriate instruments for each piece with a collection of symbols representing different instruments.
___. *Troisième recueil d'airs en duo tirés des opéra de Mrs. Rameau, Rebel et Francoeur, et autres; opéra comiques, parodies. . . choisis et ajustés pour les flûtes, violons, pardessus de violes et dont la pluspart peuvent se jouer sur la vielle et la musette.* Paris, 1758.

Boüin, François. See Methods.
___. *Les muses. Suittes à deux vielles ou musettes avec la basse; ces suittes sont gravées de façon qu'elles peuvent se jouer avec agrément sur les violons, flûte, hautbois et pardessus de violle. . . oeuvre Ier.* Paris [c.1737-1742].
Three suites for two vielles and three solo-bass suites of character pieces and dance movements. These works use the full two-octave range of the vielle and therefore are not fully playable on the musette. Transposing clefs are provided for the duos in order to make them more easily accessible by other instruments.
___. *Sonates pour la vielle et autres instruments avec la basse continue. Oeuvre 2e.* Paris [1748].
Six solo-bass works which are fundamentally French suites with a few Italianate movements. The two-octave range excludes the musette.
___. *Les amusements d'une heure et demie, contenant VI divertissements champêtres, pour violon, flûte, hautbois, pardessus de violle, vielles ou musettes, oeuvre 4e.* Paris [after 1761].
Three divertissements for two vielles and three solo-bass works.

These divertissements consist of variations on well-known melodies, such as "Ah, je vous dirai, maman" and "Les Folies d'Espagne" framed by preludes or overtures and dance movements. Transposing clefs are provided so that the pieces can be more easily played by other instruments, although the two-octave range largely eliminates the musette.

___. *Supplément au 3è recueil de contredanses nouvelles ajustées pour les vielles et musettes et le menuet d'Exaudet avec des variations.* Paris, n.d.

Bousset, René drouard de (1703-1760). *Concertos en trios pour les vieles et musettes, qui se peuvent jouer sur les flûtes traversières et à-bec, hautbois et violon. . . 1er oeuvre.* Paris, 1736.
The range of the parts makes these works playable with the violin on one part and the vielle or other melody instrument on the other. Careful dynamic markings largely eliminate the musette as an effective alternative.

Bouvard, François (1684-1760). *IIIe Receuil d'airs sérieux et à boire à une et deux voix mêlés d'ariettes, récits de basse, brunettes et vaudevilles, que l'on peut éxecuter sure les musettes et sur les vièles avec un air italien.* Paris, 1738.

Braun, Jean-Daniel (le cadet). *Deuxième oeuvre. . . contenant six suites à deux musettes qui conviennent aux vièles, flûtes à bec, traversières et hautbois.* Paris, 1728.
Six technically simple duos arranged in six suites. Suite VI is appropriate only for the musette.

Buterne, Charles. *Six sonates pour la vielle, musette, violon, flûtes, hautbois, et pardessus de violles; quatre avec la basse-continue et deux en duo. . . oeuvre IIe.* Paris [c.1745].
Four solo-bass sonatas and two unaccompanied duos. These works are technically quite difficult. Sonata No.4 uses the full two-octave range and is therefore unplayable on the musette. This book was later republished with only "B" to represent the author's name. This edition has thus been catalogued in several sources as anonymous. Modern editions: Vier Sonaten, Op.2, Heinrichshofen 2 vols., N3544, N3545 [4 solo-bass sonatas for recorder. The original of No.4 contains fingerings eliminated from the modern editions]. Zwei Duetten, Heinrichshofen N3546 [2 unaccompanied duos, Sonatas Nos.5 &6].

Charles, J. *Nouveaux amusements tendres et bacchiques. Contenants des airs à chanter, à danser, et à joüer sur le violon, la flûte, le haubois, la musette et la viéle, à I. II. et III Voix.* Paris, 1742.

Chédeville, Esprit-Philippe (1696-1762).
Members of the Chédeville family were the most prominent musette players of their time and the most prolific in the publication of compositions for that instrument. Although the majority are playable on the vielle, many works have low f sharps which preclude their performance on the latter instrument unless some suitable transposition can be found. Most collections are technically easy.
___. *Simphonies pour la musette, qui conviennent aux vielles, fluttes à bec, fluttes traversières et hautbois. Livre Ier.* Paris, 1730.
Six suites; four duos and two solo-bass.
___. *Simphonies pour la musette, qui conviennent aux vièles. . . Live II.* Paris, 1730.
Six suites; four duos and two solo-bass. Modern edition: Cinquième Suite (1730) , Billaudot.
___. *Concerts champêtres pour les musettes, vièles, flûtes et hautbois avec la basse. . . troisième oeuvre.* Paris [c.1737].
Six concerto-like trios for flute or oboe and musette with bass. One is for two musettes.
___. *Sonates pour la musette avec la basse continüe. Qui conviennent aux vielles, flûtes, hautbois, et autres instruments. . . Oeuvre IVᵉ.* Paris [1733].
Six solo-bass sonatas in the Italian style.
___. *Duos galants pour deux musettes, vièles et autres instruments. . . Cinquième oeuvre.* Paris [c.1733-1734].
Six unaccompanied duos arranged in suites. Modern edition: Sechs galante Duos, Hortus Musicus 81.
___. *Sonatilles galants pour les musettes ou vièles et autres instruments, avec la basse continüe. . . Sixième oeuvre.* Paris [1736].
Six "light" sonatas for solo-bass. A mixture of Italian and French styles. Modern edition: Sonatilles galants I-III, Heinrichshofen N3398. Facsimile edition: UCP S21.
___. *Deuxième livre de duo galants pour les musettes, vièles et autres instruments. Oeuvre 7e.* Paris [1739].
Six unaccompanied duos like the first set.
___. *Les fêtes pastorales, duos pour les musettes et vielles, et autres instruments. Oeuvre 9e.* Paris, n.d.
Six unaccompanied duos arranged as suites.

___. *Sonates pour les musettes, vielles, et autres instruments avec la basse continue. . . oeuvre Xᵉ.* Paris, n.d.
Six solo-bass sonatas.

Collections

The following collections each contain six suites made up of arrangements of the latest dances and airs by other composers, as well as Chédeville himself.

___. *[1er, 2e, 4e] Recueil de vaudevilles, menuets, contredanses et autres airs choisis pour la musette avec la basse continue qui conviennent aux vielles, fluttes, et hautbois, &c.* Paris [c.1731-1737].
Facsimile edition: 2e Receuil, UCP S75.

___. *[3e, 5e, 6e, 7e, 8e] Recueil de vaudevilles, menuets, contredanses, et autres airs choisis pour deux musettes qui conviennent aux vielles, fluttes, et hautbois, &c.* Paris [c.1734-1737].
Facsimile edition: 3e Receuil, UCP S26.

___. *Neuvième Recueil de pièces choisis et ajustées pour la musette avec la basse continue qui conviennent aux vielles, fluttes à bec.* Paris [c.1737-1742].

___. *Dixième Recueil de vaudevilles et autres airs choisis ajustés en duo pour les musettes et vielles.* Paris [after 1742].

___. *Vaudevilles, brunettes et autres airs choisis ajustés en duo pour les musettes et vièles et autres instruments. Onzième recueil.* Paris [after 1742].

___. *Nouveau Recueil de vaudevilles et autres airs choisis, ajustés en duo pour les musettes et vièles.* Paris, n.d.

___. *Recüeil de menuets ajustées, pour les musettes et vièles.* Paris [c.1734-1737].

___. *IIe Recüeil de menuets ajustées, pour les musettes et vielles.* Paris [c.1742-1751].

___. *Nouveau recueil de vaudevilles, menuets, contredanses, et autres airs choisis, ajustées en duo, pour les musettes et vielles.* Paris, 1737.

___. *[Ie-IIIe] Recueil de contredanses ajustées pour les musettes et vièles.* Ie, IIe Rec., Paris [c.1737-1742]. IIIe Rec., Paris [c.1742-1751].

___. *Nouveau recueil de noëls pour deux musettes ou vièles, flûtes, et hautbois.* Paris, n.d.

Chédeville, Nicolas (1705-1782).

___. *Amusements champêtres. Contenant trois suittes à deux musettes ou vielles et rois avec la basse continue. . . Livre premier.* Paris [1729].

Three duos and three solo-bass suites consisting of character pieces and dance movements. With the exception of the first two suites, these works are fully playable on the vielle. Facsimile edition: UCP CF42.

___. *Amusements champêtres, suittes pour la muzette, vielle, flûte traversière et hautbois . . . livre deuxième.* Paris [c.1731].

___. *Troisième livre d'amusements champêtres contenant six sonates pour la muzette, vièle, flûte traversière, hautbois et violon avec la basse continue.* Paris [c.1733].
Six solo-bass suites with programmatic titles.

___. *Les danses amuzantes mellées de vaudeville pour la muzette, vielle, flûte traversière, hautbois et violon. . . oeuvre IVe.* Paris [1733].
Six suites of pieces for two musettes or vielles of popular tunes, dances, etc.

___. *Sonates amusantes pour les muzettes, vielles, flûtes traversière, hautbois, et violons. . . Oeuvre Cinquième.* Paris [c.1733-1734].
Three solo-bass sonatas and three unaccompanied duos for Italian movements, dance movements, and character pieces. Modern edition: Fuzeau (Casteuble), Courlay.

___. *Amusements de Bellone, ou Plaisirs de Mars; pièces pour la musette, vielle, flûte et hautbois. . . Oeuvre VI.* Paris [1736].
Four "amusements" or solo-bass suites of character pieces named to commemorate the battles of fought by the Prince de Conti during his campaigns of 1733-1735.

___. *Les galanteries amusantes. Sonates à deux musettes, vielle, flûtes, vielle, flûte traversière et violon. Oeuvre 8e.* Paris [1739].
Six sonatas each with a programmatic title and comprised of four to nine character pieces. The French character of this music belies the Italian connotation of "sonata." The lower part remains consistently below the upper part and in most movements contains low F sharps. Modern edition: 2 Pastoral Sonatas Op.8, no.3, no.6, Nagels Musikarchiv 26.

___. *Les Deffis ou l'étude amusante, pièces pour la musette, ou vielle avec la basse continue. Oeuvre 9.* Paris, n.d.
A series of character pieces each with the name of a gentleman amateur. Facsimile edition: Éditions Minkoff.

___. *Les idées françoises, ou les délices de Chambray, pour deux musettes, vielles, flûtes, haubois et violons. . . Oeuvre X^e.* Paris [c.1742-1751].
Three dozen character pieces for two musettes describing the delights of the estate of Chambray.

__. *Les impromptus de Fontainebleau; pièces en deux parties, et par accord, pour les musettes, vièles, violons, pardessus de viole, flûtes traversières et hautbois. Oeuvre XIIe.* Paris, 1750.
Unaccompanied duos. The first set of pieces is named for scenes at Fontainebleau.

Unnumbered Works

__. *Les pantomimes italiennes dansées à l'Académie royale de musique mise pour la muzette, vielle, flûte traversière et hautbois par Monsieur Chédeville, Cadet, Hautbois de la Chambre du Roy.* Paris [c.1737-1742].
Four pantomimes and a collections of airs for two musettes or vielles and four solo-bass pantomimes. Pantomimes portrayed some story or dramatic action in dance. They were very popular throughout the eighteenth century, and the most famous composers and dancers worked on them. The fanciful character of this set makes them technically very difficult. They are for the most part playable on the vielle although a number are best suited to the musette. Facsimile edition: UCP S24.

__. *Nouveaux menuets champêtres pour les musettes, vièles, violons.* Paris, n.d.

__. *Le Printemps ou les saisons amusantes, concertos d'A. Vivaldi mis pour les musettes et vielles avec accompagnement de violon, flûte et Bc.* Paris [c.1737-1742].
Six concertos for musette (or vielle), violin, flute, and bass arranged from assorted movements of Vivaldi's Concertos, Op.8. Only six of the eighteen movements are from the "Four Seasons." Bröcker (see bibliography), p.318-319, has provided a table summarizing the contents of these works.

__. *Abaco Opera quarta, mis pour la musette, vielle, flûte traversière et le hautbois, avec la Bc. par Chédeville le cadet.* Paris [c.1742-1751].
Eight solo-bass sonatas from the works of Evaristo Felice Dall'Abaco (1675-1742). Although the Chédeville has attempted to remain faithful to the originals, he has added some music of his own.

__. *La feste d'Iphise. Airs de l'opéra Jephté ajustés pour deux musettes ou vielles par Mr. Chédeville le cadet.* Paris n.d.
Two dozen vocal and instrumental pieces from Montéclair's opera Jephté (1732) arranged in two suites, one in C and a shorter one in G for two musettes (some movements contain low F sharps). While accurately reproducing the melodies in the upper part, Chédeville has newly composed the second part.

__. *La Feste de Cleopâtre. Airs des festes grecques et romaines [de Colin de Blamont] Mis en deux parties égales pour les musettes et vielle.* Paris [c.1742-1751].
Collection of unaccompanied duos arranged as suites. The first provides the title for the collection. Many arrangements of works by other composers.

__. *Les Variations amusantes, pièces de différents auteurs ornées d'agréments et misses en deux parties et par accord pour les muzettes, vielles, pardessus de viole, flûtes traversières et hautbois.* Paris n.d.
Sets of variations on works by other composers beginning with twelve variations on the *Folies d'Espagne*. Since the title page is missing on some copies, this collection has been cited as a separate work under the latter title. Many of the variaitions are very elaborate with many double stops. It concludes with a suite of noels with variations.

Corrette, Gaspard (d. before 1733). *Pièces de feu M. Gaspard Corrette de Delft mises pour deux muzettes ou deux vielles. I. suite.* Paris, n.d.

Corrette, Michel (1709-1795). *VI Concerto pour les flûtes, violons, etc. . . ., le troisième est pour la muzette ou vielle. Oeuvre 4.* Paris, [c.1729].
Concerto No.3 for flute, musette, or vielle, two violins and bass is a highly effective work for any one of the three solo instruments.

__. *Pièces pour la musette, vièle, flûte à bec, flûte traversière, hautbois, dessus de viole et violon. . . oeuvre Vme.* Paris, [c.1730].
Melodically appealing character pieces and dance movements for solo and bass. Modern edition: Winterthur, Amadeus BP 378.

__. *VI fantaisies à trois parties pour la vièle et la musette, flûte et bc. qui conviennent à tous les instruments. . . Oeuvre 6.* Paris, [c.1731].
Six three-movement works which exhibit concerto-like features. The term "fantaisie" is used, imitation plays an important role. Some pieces are designated specifically for two musettes or for two vielles, but this seems to be an arbitrary selection, since occasionally low F sharps appear in parts designated for the vielle. There is one for vielle and violin and another for musette and flute.

__. *Pastorale en noëls pour les musettes, vièles, flûtes et violons, avec la basse continue. . . IIe concerto de noëls.* Paris, [c.1728-1734].
Modern edition: published for recorder by Gérard Billaudot.

__. *IIIe Concerto de noëls pour la musette . . . ce concerto peut se jouer dans l'église avec l'orgue.* Paris [c.1728-1734].
Although this work does not mention the vielle on its title page, it is

quite playable and very effective on the latter instrument.

___. *Noëls Suisses. IV. Concerto pour la musette, vièle, flûte traversière, flûte à bec, hautbois violon, pardessus de viole avec la basse continue.* Paris [c.1728-1734].
Modern edition: Amadeus BP2401.

___. *Le Berger fortuné. Concerto I° pour la musette, vièle, violon, flûte traversière, flûte à bec, hautbois, pardessus de viole avec la basse continue.* Paris [c.1734-1737].
The concertos entitled "Le Berger fortuné" are intended for musette, two violins and bass. They are, for the most part, effective for the vielle. Aside from the third concerto, which contains storms at sea, there are no programmatic effects which relate to the title. They are in the style of the Vivaldi concerto.

___. *Les Récréations du Berger fortuné. IIème Concerto pour la musette, vièle, flûte traversière, violon, flûte à bec, haut-bois, pardessus de viole avec la basse chiffrée.* Paris [c.1734-1737].

___. *Les Voyages du Berger fortuné aux Indes orientales. IIIe Concerto pour la musette, vièle, flûte, hautbois, violon, et pardessus de viole avec la basse chiffrée.* Paris [c.1734-1737].

___. *Six concerto pour trois flûtes, hautbois ou violons avec la basse. Le premier dessus du 2e, 3e, 4e, et 6e se peut jouer sur la musette et vièle. . . oeuvre VIII.* Paris, [c.1732].
This collection contains the first six concertos comiques. The four which are appropriate for the musette and vielle are listed below as they were published individually.

___. *L'Allure. IIe Concerto comique pour trois flûtes, hautbois ou violons avec la basse continue, le premier dessus se peut jouer sur la musette, vièle et flûte à bec.* Paris [c.1732].
Facsimile edition: Early Music Facsimiles (EMF #11).

___. *Margoton. IIIe Concerto comique pour trois musettes ou vièles avec la basse continue qui conviennent aux flûtes, hautbois et violons.* Paris [c.1732-1734].
Modern edition: Winterthur, Amadeus BP395 [for 3 alto recorders and bc.]

___. *L'Asne d'or. IVe Concerto pour la musette ou vielle, flûte, hautbois ou violon avec la basse travaillée d'une manière aisée pour la violoncelle.* Paris [c.1732-1734].

___. *Le Plaisir des dames. VI. Concerto comique pour les flûtes, hautbois et violons avec la basse-continue, le premier dessus se peut jouer sur la musette, vièle et flûte à bec.* Paris [by 1734].

___. *La Servante au bon tabac. VII. Concerto comique pour trois flûtes, hautbois et violons avec la basse-continue, le premier dessus se peut jouer sur la musette, vièle et flûte à bec.* Paris [by 1734].
Modern edition: Edited for recorder and published by Billaudot.

___. *Ma mie Margo. Xe Concerto comique pour la flûte, hautbois, musette, ou vièle avec deux parties de violons et la basse-continue.* Paris [c.1734-1737].

___. *La Tante Tourelourette et le Plaisir d'être avec vous. XI. Concerto comique pour la flûte, hautbois, musette ou vièle avec deux parties de violons et la basse continue.* Paris [c.1734-1737].

___. *La Découpure. XIIe Concerto comique pour la flûte, hautbois, violon, musette, vièle, pardessus de viole avec la basse continue.* Paris [c.1734-1737].

___. *La Béquille de père Barnaba. XIII. Concerto comique pour la musette, vièle, flûte, hautbois, violon, pardessus de violle avec la basse.* Paris [c.1737-1742].

___. *La Choisy. XIV. Concerto comique pour les cors de chasse, musette, vièle, flûte, violon avec la basse.* Paris [c.1737-1742].
Modern edition: Heinrichshofen 6209.

___. *Les Amours de Thérèse avec Colin. XXI. Concerto comique en pot pourri pour les musettes, vielles, violons, flûtes, hautbois, pardessus de viole avec la basse.* Paris, n.d.

Courbois, Philippe (fl.1705-1730). *Dom Quichotte, VIIe Cantate à voix seule et un violon* in *Cantates françoises à I. et II. voix. Sans simphonie et avec simphonie.* Paris, 1710.
In spite of its title, this work refers to several other instruments in the score. The last aria contains an obbligato part for the vielle. The range of the part (d'-g") would fit on a vielle in D described by Terrasson with drones in G. This is the earliest piece specifically composed for the vielle in eighteenth-century France.

Dall'Abaco, Evaristo Felice (1675-1742). See Chédeville, Nicolas.

Dampierre, Marc-Antoine, marquis de (1676-1756). *Fanfares nouvelles pour deux cors de chasse ou deux trompettes et pour les musettes, vièles et hautbois.* Paris, 1738.

Dauphin, Charles. *IVe Recueil d'airs sérieux et à boire mêlés de chansonettes et vaudevilles qui se peuvent jouer sur la flûte et musette ou vielle.* Paris, 1733.

Derochet, Louis. *Premier livre, contenant plusieurs menuets de la comédie italienne. . . Avec un debut de concerto, petite suitte pour 2 violons, flutte, musette et vielle, violoncelle ou basson, avec la basse continue.* Paris, 1732.

Dubois,___. *Le Pasteur Fidèle ou les délices de la campagne. Sonates à deux parties pour deux musettes, vielles, pardessus de viole et autres instruments. . . Oeuvre Ir.* Paris [1740].

Dugué, Philippe. *Sonates dans le goût italien pour la musette ou vièle. Avec la basse continue qui conviennent aux flûtes et autres instruments. . . Oeuvre Ir.* Paris [c.1734-1737].
A highly accomplished composer of vocal music, the Abbé Dugué, turned his compositional skill to the musette. His two sets of six solo-bass sonatas in the Italian style are equally playable on both musette or vielle, but they were intended primarily for musette.
___. *Sonates dans le goût italien pour la musette ou vièle. Avec la basse continue qui conviennent aux flûtes et autres instruments. . . Oeuvre II.* Paris [c.1734-1737].
___. *Sonates en trio pour les musettes, vièles et basse continue. . . Oeuvre IV.* Paris [c.1742-1751].
Six trio sonatas for two musettes or vielles and continuo fully playable on both instruments.

Dupuits, Jean-Baptiste (fl.1741-1757). See "methods."
___. *Première suite d'amusemens en duo. Pour les vièles, musettes, haut-bois, violons, flûtes. . . Oeuvre II.* Paris [1741].
"Pour une Viéle, ou Musette avec un Haut-bois." The following suites were published both separately and together. Although these six suites can be played with a variety of instruments, as the title page indicates, Dupuits's first preference is given above the first piece of music in each case. These are the least demanding of this composer's works.
___. *Second suite d'amusemens en duo pour les viéles, musettes, haut-bois, violons, flûtes. . . Oeuvre IIe.* Paris [1741].
"Pour deux Vielles ou Une Vielle avec une Musette ou un hautbois"
___. *Troisième suite d'amusemens en duo pour les viéles, musettes, haut-bois, violons, flûtes. . . Oeuvre IIe.* Paris [1741].
"Pour une viele et un haubois."
___. *IVe Suitte d'amusemens en duo pour les vieles, musettes, hautbois, violons, flûtes. . . Oeuvre IIe.* Paris [1741].

"Pour une viele et un haubois."

___. *Vme Suite d'amusemens en duo pour une viéle et un haubois ou autres instrumens. . . Oeuvre II.* Paris [1741].
"pour une Viele et un Haubois."

___. *Sixieme suitte d'amusemens en duo pour les vieles, musettes, haubois, flûtes, &c. . . Oeuvre II.* Paris [1741].
"Pour une Viéle et un Haubois."

___. *Sonates pour un clavecin et une vièle, laquelle partie s'exécute également sur les musettes, violons, flûtes. . . Oeuvre III.* Paris, 1741.
Sonatas for the vielle with obbligato harpsichord. Types of movements include concertos, dance movements, and fugues.

___. *Sonates ou suites à deux vièles, Oeuvre 4.* Paris, 1741.
The most difficult duos composed for the vielle. The full range of the instrument is used, and the music is idiomatic only for the vielle. This collection is notable for its audacious harmonies. Facsimile edition: UCP S6.

___. *Pièces de caractère pour la vielle. . . Oeuvre 5.* Paris, 1741.

___. *Le bouquet, cantate à voix seule avec accompagnement de vièle ou autres instruments composée par M.D.* Paris [after 1742].
Facsimile edition: Early Music Facsimile (EMF #8). This is a facsimile of the Library of Congress copy which lists only flute as accompanying instrument and is identified as anonymous.

Hotteterre, Jacques Martin (1674-1763). *Troisième suitte de pièces à deux dessus pour les flûtes traversières, flûtes-à-bec, haubois & musettes . . . oeuvre VIII.* Paris, 1722.
Hotteterre published these works before vielle was widely played as a chamber music instrument, however, they are playable and have been played on the vielle.

Hotteterre, Jean (d.1720) and Jacques Martin. *Pièces pour la muzette qui peuvent aussi se jouer sur la flûte, sur le haubois &c . . . oeuvre posthume; plus, une suitte de pièces par accords par M. Hotterre le Romain; en outre, La guerre, pièce de muzette la quelle n'a point été imprimée jusquà présent.* Paris, 1722.
This collection contains a suite of programmatic pieces entitled "The Rustic Wedding (La noce champêtre ou l'Himen pastoral)" which, although originally intended for musette has become a staple of the repertory for the vielle in recent times.Modern edition: *Die ländliche Hochzeit*, Edition Schott 2431.

Lalande, Michel Richard de (1657-1726). *Noëls en trio du feu Mr. Lalande avec un carillon pour les musettes, vielles, fluttes, violins et hautbois.* Paris [c.1734].
This edition is a direct transposition of the *Noëls en trio. . . Livre Ier* for two melody instruments and bass. The latter is available in modern editions. Although only the deuxième dessus and bass parts of this arrangement for vielle and musette survive, since it is a direct transposition of the first edition, it is possible to reconstruct the upper part.

Lavallière,___. *Six sonates en duo pour le tambourin avec un violon seul. . . suivies des principes généraux pour connoître. . . l'étendue du flûtet; et l'accord des tambourins. . . on peut exécuter ces sonates sur le haut-bois, flûte, violon et pardessus de viole, la vièle et la musette peuvent jouer le premier dessus en C sol ut.* Paris, 1749.
Music for tambourin consists of a end-blown flute accompanied by a tuned drum with ropes stretched across the head to create a rattle. It is a combination found in the folk music of southern France, but in the eighteenth century, enjoyed a short vogue as a salon instrument.

Lavigne, Philibert de. *Ier. oeuvre de Mr. de Lavigne, contenant six suites de pièces à deux musettes qui conviennent aux vièles, flûtes à bec, flûtes traversières et hautbois.* Paris, 1731.
Philibert de Lavigne was probably employed as a musette player by the Comte d'Ayen, and judging from the dedications in his works moved in the highest aristocratic circles. His first collection is a set of six easy suites playable on the vielle as well as the musette.
___. *Sonates pour la musette, vielle, flûte-à-bec, haubois, &c. avec la basse. . . IIe.Oeuvre.* Paris [c.1739].
Six sonatas for solo-bass eminently playable on the vielle. Modern edition in two volumes (each sonata also available singly): Heinrichshofen N3434, N3449.
___. *Les Fleurs. Pièces pour les musettes ou vielles, avec accompagnement de violon ou de flûte. Oeuvre 4e.* Paris [c.1742-1751].
Character pieces and dance movements for musette or vielle with an accompaniment which is most appropriate for the violin
(a number of pieces go below the range of the flute). Modern edition: Amadeus, 2 vols., GM553, GM554.

Lemaire, Jean (l'aîné). *Suite pour la vièle et la musette avec accompagnement de basse ou violon. . . oeuvre IV.* Paris, after 1751.

Expressive markings in this collection of two dozen pieces indicate that it is specifically intended for the vielle. The style is more galant than baroque. This is one of the few works that specifically eliminates the keyboard from the bass, although playing solo-bass music without harpsichord may have been a common procedure.

Lemaire, Louis (1693 or 94-c.1750). *La musette. Cantatille nouvelle avec accompag^t de musette, vielle hautbois et violons.* Paris, 1735.
Lemaire composed about 66 cantatilles most of which were first performed at the Palais du Luxembourg or the Tuileries. Two list the vielle as an alternative on the title page. This cantatille requires both musette and vielle. The latter functions in several places as an alternative to the violin parts. It also has a duet with the musette.
__. *Les plaisirs champêtres. 2me musette. Cantatille nouvelle. . . avec accompagnement de musette, vielle, flûtes, violons, &c.* Paris, 1738.
In this cantatille, the vielle is simply an alternative to the musette.

Le Marchand, __. *Six suites d'airs en duo pour le tambourin. . . 1ère oeuvre; ces duo se peuvent executer sur la vielle, la musette, flûte traversière, haubois, pardessus de viole et autres instrumens.* Paris, n.d.
__. *Nouvelle suitte d'airs pour deux tambourins, musettes ou vielles. . . lorsque l'on executera ces pièces sur la musette ou sur la vielle, l'on suposera la clef de sol sur la première ligne comme elle est marquée au commencem^t de chaque air; l'on peut aussi executer ces pièces avec une musette du cinq et un tambourin.* Paris, n.d.

Lemenu de Saint Philbert, Christophe. *Premier livre de cantatilles. Six cantatilles en symphonie.* Paris, 1742.
Contains the composer's cantatille *La Vielle* for solo vielle, soprano, and continuo.

Masse, __. *Premier (-troisième) receuil de contredanses nouvelles et anciennes ajustées pour les vielles et musettes.* Paris, n.d.

Michon, __. *Divertissements champêtres en quatre suittes avec la basse et deux dessus pour vielles, muzettes, fluttes et hautbois et autres instrumens. . . premier oeuvre.* Paris [c.1742-1751].
This composer is not to be confused (as several writers have) with a Mlle. Michon, who composed some airs in the seventeenth century. Michon's work is among the finest composed for the vielle in the eighteenth century. The first work consists of three solo-bass suites,

two in C and one in G. These suites are labelled "divertissement" which calls attention to their orchestral features. There is also an unaccompanied suite en duo for vielle and musette. Although this combination was probably common, this suite is unique in its specific directions for this combination.

___. *Amusemens de chambre avec la basse continue et une sonatte dans le goût italien et une suitte en duo pour vieille[!], musette et autres instrumens. . . second oeuvre.* Paris [c.1742-1751].

As the title indicates, this work begins with an extensive suite of dances followed by a sonata with both French and Italian characteristics. These are followed by a suite for two vielles. These works are notable for their harmonic richness, tuneful melodies and features of the incipient galant style.

Montéclair, Michel Pignolet de (1667-1737). See Nicolas Chédeville.

___. *Troisième concert dessus & basse, par Mr Montéclair[.] Les airs qui composent ce troisième concert conviennent à la musette, à la vielle, au haubois, au violon, au dessus de violle, a la flûte-traversière, et à la flûte-à-bec.* Paris, 1724.

Found in the *Concerts pour la flûte traversière avec la basse chiffrée,* this work requires considerable adaptation for performance on the vielle, since it is filled with double stops and low F sharps.
Facsimile edition: Florence, Archivum Musicum 11.

Naudot, Jacques-Christophe (c.1690-1762). *VIIe oeuvre contenant six sonates et un caprice en trio pour deux flûtes traversières, violons et hautbois, avec la basse dont il y a en a trois qui peuvent se jouer sur musettes, vièles et flûtes à bec. . .* Paris [c.1731-1734].

The premier dessus of Sonata II (G), Sonata IV (G), and VI (C) are playable on the vielle (or musette). The deuxième dessus is playable only on the transverse flute, violin, and oboe.

___. *Huitième oeuvre de Mr Naudot, contenant six Fêtes rustiques pour les musettes, vièles, flutes, haubois, & violons, avec la basse. . .* Paris [c.1731-1734].

These works are trios for a drone instrument (musette or vielle) and a melody instrument (flute, oboe, or violin). Two of them are unplayable on the vielle due to low F sharps. Of the four remaining, two listed below are available in modern edition. These trios have concerto-like features which contrast the melody and drone instruments, providing solos for each. Modern edition: Trio I, Schott Antiqua, vol.82. Trio III, Edition Schott 5360.

___. *Dixiéme oeuvre contenant VI. babioles pour II. vièles, musettes, flûtes-à-bec, flûtes traversières, haubois ou violons, sans basse.* Paris, [c.1737].
Six suites of character pieces and dance movements. These works are among the best duos suitable for the vielle. Modern edition: Edition Schott, 2 vols., 5734, 5735.

___. *XIVᵉ oeuvre, contenant six sonates pour une vièle avec la basse, dont trois sont mêlées d'accord. . .* Paris [c.1737-1742].
Six difficult solo-bass works modelled on the sonata da chiesa. The last three sonatas exploit double stops more thoroughly than any other composer for the vielle.

___. *XVIIᵉ oeuvre. . . contenant sonates en quatre parties pour les vièles, musettes, flûtes traversières, flûtes à bec et hautbois, 2 violons et basse. . .* Paris, [c.1740-1742].
Although fully playable by the instruments listed on the title page, these works are dedicated to the legendary vielle virtuoso Danguy. Along with the concertos of Corrette, they are the only true concertos for the vielle. Modern edition: Concerto No.2, Edition Schott 5680. Concerto No.4 in G Major, Hortus Musicus 153.

___. *Divertissement champêtre en trio, pour musette ou vièle une flûte et un violon. . .* Paris, 1749.
The instrumentation of this trio and the following for musette or vielle, flute and violin unaccompanied is unique in the repertory. They are also highly effective. These trios are suites with dance movments and character pieces.

___. *Les plaisirs de Champigny ou Suite en trio pour une musette ou vièle, une flûte et un violon.* Paris [c.1742-1751].

Piffet le cadet, [Joseph Antoine?]. *Sonates en duo pour le violon qui peuvent se jouer sur la musette et vielle.* Paris, n.d.
These works can be played as duos with musette or vielle and violin. The range of the upper part is appropriate to the former instruments, while the lower part is quite idiomatic for the violin with its extensive use of the lower strings and multiple stops.

Prieur, ___. *Premier oeuvre contenant six suites de pièces pour la musette ou vielle avec la basse continue; qui conviennent aux flûtes, et hautbois, etc.* Paris [c.1734-1737].
Six technically modest suites of dance movements equally playable on musette or vielle.

Prudent, ___ (d.c.1780). *Les bouquets de Chassenay. Pour la viele, musette et dessus de viole avec accompagnement de basse et violon.* Paris [c.1742-1751].

This work contains four solo-bass sonatas and two for violin and vielle. This work fully exploits the two-octave range and is noteworthy for its extensive use of counterpoint.

Ravet, __. *Suittes et sonates à deux vièles et avec la basse continue. Livre Ier.* Paris [c.1737-1742].

Three unaccompanied duos and three solo-bass sonatas.

__. *Sonates pour la vielle qui conviennent aux musettes, flûtes, hautbois & violons. Oeuvre IIe.* Paris [c.1742-1751].

This work contains five solo-bass sonatas each with a programmatic title and three duos for vielle and violin. Virtuosity consists of rapid scale passages and double stops.

Senaillié, Jean Baptiste (c.1688-1730). *Sonates. . . ajustées pour les musettes et vielles.* Amsterdam [c.1735].

One of the few works for the musette and vielle published outside France. It contains sixteen sonatas selected and transcribed from Senallié's five books of solo-bass sonatas published between 1710 and 1727. These transcriptions depart considerably from the originals and even include new movements. They are, however, quite effective for the musette and vielle and have been designed to work for both instruments. Parts which go too high for the musette are provided with an alternate passage in a lower range.

Spourni, Wenceslaus Joseph. *VI Sonates pour une musette ou vielle, violon et basse. . . oeuvre 6.* Paris [c.1741-1742].

Although these works are playable on both musette and vielle, they are clearly intended for the former. In spite of vigorous Italianate themes, these works are harmonically unadventurous.

Tolou, A. *VI Sonates pour les musettes et vielles, avec une flûte seule. . . livre premier.* Paris, 1741.

Duos with an upper part for the flute and a lower part for musette or vielle. Although these works are fully playable on the vielle, they are quite difficult to realize musically.

Vivaldi, Antonio (1678-1741) (pseud.). *Il pastor fido, sonates pour la musette, vielle, flûte, hautbois, violon, avec la basse continue. Opera XIIIa.* Paris, [c.1737].

Arguably the best known works in this literature because of their attribution to a well-known name. The individual movements of these sonatas are in fact arrangements of works by Vivaldi and others or at least based on themes by them. Modern edition: Hortus Musicus 135.

Voyenne, __. *Six suittes de simphonies pour deux musettes ou vielles. Elles ce[!] peuvent ausi[!] exécuter sur les violons flûtes et hautbois . . . livre premier.* Paris [c.1737-1742].

II Methods (see also "Manuscripts")

Ballard, Jean-Baptiste Christophe Ballard (1663-1750). *Pièces choisies pour la vielle à l'usage des commençants avec des instructions pour toucher, & pour entretenir cet instrument.* Paris, 1732, new edition, 1742.

Bordet, Toussaint. *Méthode raisonnée pour apprendre la musique d'une façon plus claire et plus précise à laquelle on joint l'étendue de la flûte traversière, du violon, du pardessus de viole, de la vielle et de la musette, leur accord, quelques observations sur la touche desdits instruments et des leçons simples, mésurées et variées, suivies d'un recueil d'airs en duo faciles et connus pour la plus-part. Livre Ier.* Paris [1755].

Boüin, François. *La Vielleuse habile, ou nouvelle méthode courte, très facile et très sure pour apprendre à jouer de la vielle. . . oeuvre IIIe.* Paris, 1761.
Facsimile edition: Éditions Minkoff (together with Dupuits).

Corrette, Michel (1709-1795). *La belle vielleuse, méthode pour apprendre facilement, à jouer de la vielle, contenant des leçons ou les doigts sont marqués pour les commençans; avec des jolis airs et ariettes en duos deux suittes avec la basse et des chansons.* Paris, 1783.
An earlier version of this work may have been published as early as 1763 but is not extant.
Facsimile editions: (1) Saint-Denis-le Gast: Musiciens et Musique en Normandie, supplément, J.-F. Détrée, directeur, 1978. Introduction by Claude Flagel.
(2) Éditions Minkoff, 1984.

Dupuits, Jean-Baptiste (fl.1741-1757). *Principes pour toucher de la vièle avec six sonates pour cet instrument qui conviennent aux violon, flûte, clavecin, &c. . . Oeuvre Ir.* Paris, 1741.

Facsimile edition: Éditions Minkoff (together with Boüin).

III Music for the Vielle in Stage Works

Brou,__. *La Noce de village. Ballet pantomime dansée sur le theâtre de l'Opera Comique foire St. Germain, le vingt^{me}, ce qui peut s'exécuter sur la flûte, vielles [ou] musette, avec la basse continue, et pareillement utile pour les troupes de comédie en province.* Paris [1741].
A collection of dances in D minor and major.   They must be transposed and altered to be played on the vielle.

Chauvon, François. *Les Agréments champêtres. Pastorale. . . ce divertissement est à grand choeur, avec simphonies pour les violons, flûtes, hautbois, trompettes, tambourins, musettes, vielles, cors-de-chasse, violles, violoncelles.* Paris, 1736.
This work contains sections where vielles and musettes accompany choral passages.

Lully, Jean, Baptiste (1632-1687). *Ballet de l'impatience*, LWV 14 [Presented February 19, 1661].
Quatrième partie, III. Entrée des aveugles.
__. *Hercule amoureux*, LWV 17 [Presented February 7, 1662].
Lully composed for this tragedy the *Ballet des sept planètes*. The X. Entrée contains a scene entitled, "Pour les pellerins jouant de la vielle."

Mouret, Jean-Joseph (1682-1738). *Le Philosophe trompé par la nature*. Paris, c.1726.
This work was first presented at the Comédie de Saint Jorry in 1725. The music is found in the composer's collection of music from the fair theaters *Premier recueil des divertissements du mouveau theâtre italien augmenté de toutes les simphonies, accompagnemens airs de violons, de flûtes, de hautbois, de musettes, airs italiens et de plusieurs divertissemens qui n'ont jamais paru.*

Rameau, Jean-Philippe. *Les fêtes de l'Hymen et de l'Amour, ou les Dieux d'Egypt. Ballet héroïque en trois entrées et un prologue.* [Presented March 15, 1747.]
Vielles and musettes are doubled and accompany the chorus in what is meant to be an overwhelming conclusion.

IV Manuscripts

Paris, Bibliotheque de l'Arsenal, Ms.2547.
    Prepared for a provincial official around 1740, this manuscript
    contains (approximately) 473 arrangements of the most popular pieces
    of music of the period arranged for the vielle alone or in duo for two
    unaccompanied vielles. These pieces can be categorized as (1) works
    by individual composers, (2) Popular songs, (3) noëls, (4) fanfares and
    other works for trumpets, and (5) dances. The largest single group is
    149 menuets. Among the composer included are Lully, Montéclair,
    Marin and Roland Marais, Louis de Caix d'Hervelois, Forqueray,
    François Couperin, Rebel, Duval, Destouches.   The manuscript
    contains over a dozen pieces by Danguy, the only surviving works of
    this legendary player. Bröcker, p.315-316, discusses this manuscript
    without citing its location.

Paris, Bibliotheque Nationale, Ms.Vm^{7}3643, "Receuil de Contredanses
    transposée[s] pour la vielle."
    This manuscript of 383 pages contains over 800 arrangements of well-
    known melodies for vielle and bass.   For incipits, see Jules
    Ecorcheville, *Catalogue*, vol.5.

Paris, Bibliothèque National, Cons. Rés. 1177. "Airs pour la viele avec les
    principes généraux."
    This manuscript is a draft of a method which was never published.
    It consists of an instructional section and a selected group of
    arrangements of works by other composer, such as Handel and
    Geminiani. It also includes the anonymous author's variations on
    these arrangements. The many blank pages which were probably
    projected to be additonal pieces testify to its incomplete state.

Paris, Bibliothèque Nationale, Cons. L.12.867. "Recueil d'airs pour la
    vielle."

    Collection of airs, dances and assorted pieces without accompaniment
    orignally from the library of Mme. de Senozan.

V Unlocated Works

There are three sources for the following list: (1) the composer's catalogue of his works as found at the beginning of one of his publications (2) advertisements in the *Mercure de France* and (3) publisher's catalogues. The latter two sources are tabulated by Anik Devriès (see bibliography). Given below is a composer, approximate title, an approximate date, and the most accurate source of a date.

Anon. Etrennes: Solo pour les musettes et vielles. Paris [c.1737-1742]. Leclerc catalogue, 1742.

Anon. La Feste d'Angélique: Solo pour les musettes et vielles. Paris [c.1742-1751]. Leclerc catalogue, 1751.

Anon. Principes de vielles et pièces choisies. Paris, 1734. Leclerc catalogue, 1734.

Besozzi, Alexandre. Concerto pour les musettes et vielles: Les Festes champêtres. Paris [c.1742-1751]. Leclerc catalogue, 1751.

Boismortier, Joseph Bodin de. Six sonatas for vielle, musette or other instruments and bass, Op.77. Paris, c.1737. Composer's catalogue.
__. Quatre gentilesses for musettes, vielles or other instruments and bass, Op.79. Paris, c.1740. Composer's catalogue.
__. Six sonates en trio for vielles, musettes or other instruments and bass, Op.96. Paris, c.1741. Composer's catalogue.
__. Duo for musette or vielle and violin, Op.101. Paris, after 1741. Composer's catalogue.

Bourgeois, Louis. Trio pour les musettes et vielles: Ière Suitte. Paris [1742-1751]. Leclerc catalogue, 1751.

Buterne, Charles. Solo pour les musettes et vielles, Premier livre. Paris [1742-1751]. Leclerc catalogue, 1751.

Chauvet, Etienne-Siméon. Duo pour les musettes et vielles: Ier livre. Paris [1742-1751]. Leclerc catalogue, 1751.

Colini (Mlle). Pièces pour les musettes et vielles: Quatre livres de menuets. Paris [1734-1737]. Leclerc catalogue, 1737.

Cordelet, Claude. Solo pour les musettes et vielles: 1er et 2eme livre.

Paris [1742-1751]. Leclerc catalogue, 1751.

D. Concerto comique par D. . . pour les musettes et vielles. Paris [c.1737-1742]. Leclerc catalogue 1742.
These works are not by Dupuits, since they appear in the same catalogue which advertises his works.
___. Pièces pour les musettes et vielles par D. 1er livre en duo. Paris [c.1737-1742]. Leclerc catalogue, 1742.
___. Solo pour les musettes et vielles. 1er livre par D. Paris [c.1737-1742]. Le clerc catalogue, 1742.

David, François. Duo pour les musettes et vielles: premier livre. Paris [c.1751]. Leclerc catalogue, 1751.

Derochet, Louis. Pièces pour les musettes et vielles: Menuets et plusieurs airs. Paris [1734-1737]. Leclerc catalogue, 1737.
___. Concerto Le Jaloux. Paris [1737]. *Mercure de France*, June, 1737, p.1397-1398.
___. Duo pour les musettes et vielles: 2e livre. Paris [1737-1742]. Leclerc catalogue, 1742.
___. Les Nouvelles Bagatelles. Paris [1740]. *Mercure de France*, December, 1740, p.2917-2919.

Deshayes, Claude. Premier livre de sonates pour deux flûtes traversières, et qui conviennent au violon, hautbois, viele et musette en ravalement. Paris [1731]. *Mercure de France*, April, 1731.

Filosarti, ___. Concerto pour les musettes et vielles. Paris [1742-1751]. Leclerc catalogue, 1751.

Gianotti, Pietro. Duo pour les musettes et vielles: 8e livre. Paris [1742-1751]. Leclerc catalogue, 1751.
___. Trio pour les musettes et vielles: 14e livre. Paris [1751-1753]. Leclerc catalogue, 1753.
___. Les Petits Concerts de Daphnis et Chloé. Paris [1760-1762]. Leclerc catalogue, 1762.
___. Les Soirées de Limiel. Paris [c.1762]. Leclerc catalogue, 1760-1762.
___. Les Soirées de Boulevard. Paris [1764]. *L'Avant-Coureur*, November 19, 1764.
___. Les Vendanges de Sologne. Paris [1764]. *L'Avant-Coureur*, November 19, 1764.

Giardini, Felice. Concerto pour les musettes et vielles: Concerto comique. Paris [1742-1751]. Leclerc catalogue, 1751.

Guillemain, Louis Gabriel. Pièces pour deux vielles, musettes, flûtes ou violon, Op.9. Paris [c.1741]. Composer's catalogue.
__. Simphonies d'un goût nouveau en forme de concerto pour les musettes vielles, flûtes ou hautbois, Op.16. Paris [1752]. Composer's catalogue.

Guillon, Henri Charles. Duo pour les musettes et vielles: 1er livre. Paris [1737-1742]. Leclerc catalogue, 1742.
__. Duo, 2e livre. Paris [1744]. *Mercure de France*, February, 1744.

Lavigne, Philibert de. Trios pour les musettes et vielles: 3e Livre. Paris [c.1737-1742]. Leclerc Catalogue, 1742.

Lemaire, Jean (l'aîné). Duo, musettes et vielles: 3e livre. Paris [1742-1751]. Leclerc catalogue, 1751.

Lemaire, Louis (1693 or 94-c.1750). Fanfares ou concerts de chambre pour violon, flûte, hautbois, musette et vielle. Paris, 1741.

P. Principes pour la vielle par M. P. Paris [c.1737-1742]. Leclerc catalogue, 1742.

Petit, __. Solo pour les musettes et vielles: 1er livre de menuets. Paris [1737-1742]. Leclerc catalogue, 1742.

Prota, Tomaso. Trio pour les musettes et vielles: 1er livre. Paris [1737-1742]. Leclerc catalogue, 1742.

Rameau, Jean Philippe. Duo pour les musettes et vielles (de pièces recueillies des opéras): 1er livre. Paris [1737-1742]. Leclerc catalogue, 1742.
__. 2e livre. Paris [c.1750]. *Mercure de France*, January, 1750. p.186.

Spourni, Wenceslas. Solo pour les musettes et vielles: 1ère suitte. Paris [1742-1751]. Leclerc catalogue, 1751.
__. Duo pour les musettes et vielles: 1ère suitte, 16e livre. Paris [c.1743]. Leclerc catalogue, 1744.
__. Différents musiques pour les vielles et musettes: Concertino 4e. Paris [c.1743]. Leclerc catalogue, 1744.

APPENDIX

Avertissements in the Works of Jean-Baptiste Dupuits

Sonates pour un Clavecin et une Vièle (1741)

Avertissement

Although there seems to be much difficulty uniting a harpsichord with a vielle because of the natural contrast which exists between the two instruments, the few modulations which the vielle permits have been my greatest difficulty. I have made these pieces in a way that the harpsichord and the vielle can shine equally, which will be easy to see in each movement where I have designated with the word "solo" the places which are made for each of these instruments. Not only have I used all my efforts to produce new and diverse melodies as much as the accompaniment of the vielle would allow me, but further I have observed that these sonatas can be executed on the violin, the flute and the musette. With regard to this latter instrument, I have marked with little notes an octave below those passages which go out of its range, and in places where a guidon will be found with notes above or below one or another of these letters, for example A, B, C, etc. It is for the violin or the flute that I have put the mark in order to continue or take the notes an octave lower, which is their true position, having been obliged to transpose them, the [range of] the vielle not passing the lower G.

I preferred to give the highest notes to the vielle and to keep the right hand of the harpsichord around the middle of the keyboard in order to separate more the two instruments one from the other. Most of the pieces which make up these sonatas can be executed on the vielle without the accompaniment of the harpsichord, such as many of the detached movements, which will be easily seen by the menuets, the musettes, the gavottes the rondeaux, &c. These sonatas can be executed as well on the harpsichord alone, however more cautiously. [In] all movements of sustained melody, such as the Canon, the Allegro of Sonata No.2, the minuets, musettes, gavottes, rondeaux, with the exception of the Rondeau, page 4, it is necessary to play the part of the vielle with the right hand, omitting the part written for this hand which is often only a figural accompaniment, and to play the bass without any change.

I believed it necessary to compose these pieces in this way, because the vielle not being an instrument [which can be] perfectly softened, the principal melody which would be played by the right hand of the harpsichord would be found to be too absorbed. Also entire movements for the harpsichord will be recognized by the word "solo" written at the beginning of the piece in the part for this instrument. With regard to other movements where the melody alternates [between the two parts], it is necessary in the places where figures are found (which are nothing else than ordinary accompaniment) to take the part of the vielle at the beginning of the word "solo" until the melody returns to the right hand.

In order to reconcile these instruments more perfectly, the vielle, if it is constructed in the body of a lute, must be small and much softened. If it is in the body of a guitar, it must not have more sound than the old guitars.[1] For this effect, the strings must rest lightly and evenly on the wheel, only the chanterelles [should be] thicker than the trompette, without more force [on the wheel], articulate the notes only with the fingers avoiding perpetual *coups de poignet* if it is not absolutely required, such as at the beginning of a piece, the beginnings and ends of each reprise. As few vielles have an F sharp at the high end of the clavier (which is very necessary especially if one plays in G), in order to execute those movements called fugue and canon, the F must be tuned a semitone higher than it is set in ordinary claviers.[2] If some place is found where the fingering, the different *coups de poignet*, or the ornaments are difficult, just consult my First Work [Dupuit's method] where one will find the difficulties cleared up.

I am persuaded that in paying attention to the measures I have given, one will be bound to do justice to the effect of these two instruments, since they will be perfectly united with each other. It is only after several tests with I have made with Monsieur Danguy that I venture to present to the public a work the newness of which I hope it will appreciate.

[Quoiqu'il paroisse beaucoup de difficulté d'unir un Clavecin avec une Viéle par le contraste naturel qu'il y a entre ces deux Instruments, le peu de Modulations que permet la Viéle a été mon plus grand embarras.

J'ay pratiqué ces piéces de façon que le Clavecin et la Viéle peuvent y briller également ce qui sera aisé de voir dans chaque morçeau où J'ay

---

[1]By 1741, makers were building guitar-shaped instruments which were much larger than the instruments built on the bodies of real guitars. These instruments were therefore much louder.

[2]Vielles have only one key for F and F sharp, It is probably most often used as F natural, but several composers call for the high F sharp requiring the retuning of this note before playing.

désigné par le mot Solo les endroits qui sont faits pour chacun de ces Instruments. Non seulement J'ay fait tous mes efforts pour produire des chants nouveaux et diversifiés autant que l'accompagnement de la Viéle a pû me le permettre, mais encore j'ay observé que ces sonates puissent s'éxécuter sur le Violon, la Flûte et la Musette, à l'égard de ce dernier Instrument j'ay marqué par de petites Notes, à l'Octave d'en bass les passages qui passent son étenduë, et dans les endroits où on trouvera un Guidon avec des Notes au dessus ou seulement au dessous l'une ou l'autre de ces lettres sçavoir a, b, c, &c c'est pour le Violon ou la Flûte que j'ay mis cette marque pour continuer ou prendre ces notes une Octave plus bas le Sol d'en bas.

J'ay mieux aimé donner les chants superieurs à la Viéle et tenir la main droite du Clavecin vers le milieu du Clavier, pour plus détacher ces Instruments l'un de l'autre. La plûpart des piéces qui composent ces Sonates peuvent s'éxécuter sur la Viéle, sans l'accompagnement du clavecin, comme autant de morçeaux détachés ce qu'on verra aisément par les Menuets, les Musettes, les Gavottes, les Rondeaux &c. Ces Sonates s'executent également sur le Clavecin seul, cependant avec plus de précaution. Tous les morçeaux de Chants suivis comme le Canon, l'Allegro de la 2ᵉ Sonate, les Menuets, Musettes, Gavottes, Rondeaux, à l'Exception du Rondeau page 4, il faut toucher la partie de la Viéle de la main droite, en obmettant la partie écrite pour cette main qui souvent n'est qu'un accompagnement figuré, et toucher la Basse sans aucun changement.

J'ay cru devoir composer ces piéces de cette façon parce que la Viéle n'étant pas parfaitement adouci, le Chant principal qu'auroit touché la main droite au Clavecin se seroit trouvé trop absorbé. Il est aussi des morçeaux entiers pour le Clavecin ce que l'on connoitra par le solo écrit au commencement de la piéce, à la partie de cet Instrument, à l'égard des autres morçeaux dont le Chant est alternatif, il faut dans les endroits où il se trouvera des chiffres (ce qui n'est autre chose que de l'accompagnement ordinaire) prendre la partie de la Viéle au commencement du mot Solo, jusqu'à ce que le Chant reprenne dans la partie de la main droite.

Pour concilier ces Instruments plus parfaitement il est necessaire que la Viéle, si elle est construite en corps de Luth, soit petite et beaucoup adoucir, si elle est en corps de Guitarre qu'elle n'ait pas plus de jeu que ces anciennes Guitarres, pour cet effet que les cordes portent légérement et également sur la roüe, seulement les chanterelles plus grosse que la Trompette sans porter d'avantage, ne détacher les notes que des doigts, et non pas des coups de poignet perpetuels, si ce n'est celles qui semblent

Trompette sans porter d'avantage, ne détacher les notes que des doigts, et non pas des coups de poignet perpetuels, si ce n'est celles qui semblent l'éxiger absolument comme le début d'une piéce, les commencements et les fins de chaque reprise.

Comme peu de Viéles ont un Futfa diése au haute du Clavier, (ce qui est trés nécessaire surtout lorsqu'on joüe dans le mode de Grésol) pour éxécuter les morçeaux appellés Fugue, & Canon, il faut accorder ce fa un demi ton plus haut qu'il n'est monté dans les Claviers ordinaires. S'il se trouve quelqu'endroit difficile soit pour l'ordre des doigts, soit pour les différents coups de poignet, soit pour les agréments il ny a qu'a consulter mon premier Oeuvre où l'on trouvéra ces difficultés levées.

Je suis persuadé qu'en faisant attention aux moyens que je viens de donner, on sera obligé de rendre justice à l'effet de ces deux Instruments, lorsqu'ils seront parfaitement unis entr'eux, ce n'est qu'apréci plusieurs épreuves que j'ay faites avec Monsieur Danguy que je hazarde de présenter au Public un ouvrage dont je souhaite qu'il goûte la nouveauté.

Pièces de caractères Pour la Vielle. . . Oeuvre V (1741)

Avertissement

The new pieces which I give to the public are of a type such as there are few for this instrument. The execution of them is not more easy than that of my other works. Their difficulties are not so much in extraordinary [hand] positions, but in the particular characters which each has which must be rendered with the necessary exactitude. I have composed these pieces here in a way that they can be executed without the thoroughbass, however, their characters will be rendered precisely only when the two parts are together. It is very important that the accompanimental part (which is the bass) be executed with as much care as if it were the principal part. These pieces will go better without the harpsichord, although I have figured the bass, because some place is always found where a delicate ear is not satisfied by the correctness of the figures or the precision of the accompanist. I have taken care to put in each piece the necessary ornaments according to the character indicated, and although [the pieces] are susceptible to many others, the fewer that might be supplied [by the player], the better. I mixed pieces with different musical characteristics[3] for the amusement of everyone. A tender piece executed

---

[3]Dupuits uses the word *mouvements* here which refers to the tempos and gestures which

with delicacy and taste is preferable to a piece which has for all its worth only a great volubility from which there remains nothing after having heard it except surprise. It should be noted that in order to render the character of *La Labyrinthe* on page 38 , which is composed of two rondeaux and two minuets intertwined with each other, there should not be any interruption in the execution of these four sections which are all different.

Several passages made up of double notes, one above the other, will be found in these pieces, as in the second part of *La Dupuits*, page 42, line 11, measure 1-7. These are nothing more than perpetual trills which create the effect of a broken chord played very quickly. They are played by holding the lower note and beating the upper note like an ordinary trill, but without any appoggiatura or preparation.

I ask that all those who will wish to play these pieces to sin more by [playing them] too slowly than too quickly, because after having practiced them several times, the true tempo will imperceptibly be grasped. I have used the same ornament [signs] as in my other works. If some are found which are puzzling, an explanation of them will be found in my book *Principes pour toucher de la viele*. Besides it will always indeed be my pleasure to make myself helpful to people who do me the honor of consulting me either for the vielle or the harpsichord and other musical difficulties. For this purpose I will be available three days a week.

[Les nouvelles pieces que je donne au public sont d'une espece comme il en est peu pour cet instrument. L'execution n'en est pas plus facile que celle de mes autres Oeuvres; ce n'est pas tant dans des positions extraordi-naires que consiste leurs difficultés, que dans les caracteres qu'elles ont chacunes en particulier, lesquels il faut rendre avec toute l'exactitude necessaire. J'ay Composé toutes ces pieces de façon qu'elles pouront s'executer sans la Basse Continued, cependant leurs caracteres ne seront precisément rendus que quand les deux parties seront ensemble; il importe beaucoup que la partie d'accompagnement (qui est la Basse) soit executée avec autant d'attention comme si c'etoit la partie principale. Ces pieces feront mieux sans Clavecin quoique j'aye chiffré la Basse, car quelqu'exactitude qu'il y ait dans les chiffres ou de precision dans l'accompagnateur; il se trouve toujours quelqu'endroit ou une oreille delicatte n'est pas fort satisfaitte. J'aye eu soin de mettre à chaque piece les agrements necessaires suivant le caractere qu'elle doit designer et quoiqu'elles soit susceptibles de beaucoup d'autres, le moins qu'on pourra

---

help to create the character of the individual piece. In other places in this introduction, he uses the same word to refer specifically to tempo.

suppleer sera le mieux. J'ay melé des pieces de differents mouvements pour l'amusement de tout le monde; une piece tendre executée avec delicatesse, avec goute, est suivant moy plus a preferer qu'une piece qui n'a pour tout merite qu'une grande volubilité, et laquelle il ne reste rien apres l'avoir entendu que la surprise. Il faut observer pour rendre le caractere du labyrinthe page 38, qui est composé de deux Rondeaux et de deux Menuets entrelassés l'un dans l'autre, de ne mettre aucune interuption dans l'execution de ces quatre morceaux dont les mouvements doivent tous etre differents. On trouvera dans ces pieces plusieurs passages de double nottes les unes sur les autres, comme dans la seconde parties de la Dupuits page 42, ligne 11e. mesure 1re. jusqu'a la septieme; ce n'est autre chose que les cadences perpetuelles qui font l'effet d'une batterie tres vive. Elles se font entenant la notte de dessous et battre celle de dessus precisément de meme qu'une cadence battuë a l'ordinaire sans aucun appui n'y aucune preparation.

Je prie tous ceux qui voudront executer ces pieces d'y pecher plutôt par le trop de lenteur que par le trop de vivacité, parcequ'insensiblement apres les avoir repeté plusieurs fois, on en saisi le veritable mouvment. Je me suis servi des memes agrements que dans mes autres ouvrages; s'il s'en trouve quelqu'uns qui embarasse on en trouvera l'explication dans mon livre de principes pour toucher de la Viele; d'ailleurs je me feray toujours un vrai plaisir d'etre utile aux personnes qui me feront l'honneur de me consulter tant pour la Viele, que le Clavecin et autres difficultés de Musique, a cet effet on me trouvera trois jours de la semaine.]

BIBLIOGRAPHY

Primary Sources

Anon. "Lettre écrite de Paris le 29. juillet 1738 sur les memoires pour servir à l'histoire de musique." *Mercure de France*, August, 1738: 1721-1736.

Anon. "Memoires pour servir à l'Histoire de la musique vocale et instrumentale." *Mercure de France*, June, 1738: 1110-1118.

Anon. *Tablettes de renommée des musiciens, auteurs, compositeurs, virtuoses, amateurs et maîtres de musique vocale et instrumentale, les plus connus en chaque genre . . . Pour servir à l'Almanach Dauphin.* Paris, 1785. Rpt. Geneva: Éditions Minkoff, 1971.

Bâton, Charles. Mémoire sur la vielle en D-la-ré." *Mercure de France* October 1752: 143-157.

Borjon de Scellery, Charles E. *Traité de la musette avec une nouvelle méthode pour apprendre de soy-mesme à jouer de cet instrument facilement, & en peu de temps.* Lyon: Giran & Riviere, 1672.

Campion, François. *Lettre de Monsieur l'Abbé Carbasus à Monsieur de *** auteur du Temple du Goust, sur la mode des instrumens de musique, ouvrage curieux & interressant pour les amateurs de l'harmonie.* Paris: la Veuve Allouel, 1739.

Diderot, Denis, ed. *Encyclopédie ou dictionnaire raisonné des sciences, des arts et des métiers par une société de gens de lettres.* Neufchastel: Chez Samuel Faulche & Compagnie, 1751-1780.

LeBlanc, Hubert. *Défense de la basse de viole contre les entreprises du violon et les prétensions du violoncel.* Amsterdam: Pierre Mortier, 1740. Trans. by Barbara Garvey Jackson. *Journal of the Viola da Gamba Society of America* 10 (1973): 11-28, 11 (1974): 17-59, 12 (1975): 14-36.

Mersenne, Marin. *Harmonie universelle.* Paris: Chez Sebastien Cramoisy, 1636. Rpt. Paris: Éditions du C.N.R.S., 1975.

Terrasson, Antoine de. *Dissertation historique sur la vielle.* Paris: J.B. Lamesle, 1741. Rpt. Amsterdam: Antiqua, 1966.

___. *Mélanges d'histoire, de littérature, de jurisprudence litteraire, de critique.* Paris: Chez la veuve Simon & fils, 1768.

Trichet, Pierre. "Le traité des instruments de musique de Pierre Trichet." François Lesure, ed. *Annales Musicologiques* 3 (1955): 283-387, 4 (1956): 175-248.

Secondary Sources

Barnes, Clifford R. "Instruments and Instrumental Music at the 'Théatres de la Foire'." *Recherches* 5 (1965): 142-168.

Benoit, Marcelle, *Versailles et les musiciens du roi. Étude institutionelle et sociale (1661-1733).* Paris: Éditions A. et J. Picard, 1971.

___, ed. *Dictionnaire de la musique en France aux XVIIe et XVIIIe siècles.* Paris: Fayard, 1992.

Bono, Marcello. *La Ghironda. Storia, repertorio, tecnica esecutiva e costruzione.* Tradizioni Musicali 5. Bologna: Arnaldo Forni Edition, 1989.

Brenet, Michel. *Les concerts en France sous l'ancien régime.* Paris: Librairie Fischbacher, 1900. Rpt. New York: Da Capo Press, 1970.

Bröcker, Marianne. *Die Drehleier: Ihr Bau und ihre Geschichte.* 2nd ed. 3 vols. Orpheus-Schriftenreihe zu Grundfragen der Musik 11. Düsseldorf: Verlag der Gesellschaft zur Förderung der systematischen Musikwissenschaft, 1977.

Brossard, Yolande de. *Musiciens de Paris 1535-1792. Actes d'état civil d'après le fichier Laborde de la Bibliothèque Nationale. Vie musicale en France sous les rois Bourbons 11.* Paris: Éditions A. et J. Picard, 1965.

Bruni, A. *Un inventaire sous la terreur. État des instruments de musique relevé chez les émigrés et condamnés par A. Bruni, l'un des délegués de la Convention.* J. Gallay, ed. Paris: Georges Chamerot, 1890.

Chassaing, Jean-François. *La vielle et les luthiers de Jenzat.* Combronde: Aux Amoureux de Science, 1987.

Constant, Pierre. *Histoire du Concert Spirituel 1725-1790*. Paris: Société Française de Musicologie, Heugel et Cⁱᵉ, 1975.

Cucuel, Georges. *La Pouplinière et la musique de chambre au XVIIIᵉ siècle.* Paris: Librairie Fischbacker, 1913. Rpt. New York: Da Capo Press, 1971.

Devriès, Anik. *Édition et commerce de la musique gravée à Paris dans la première moitié du XVIIIᵉ siècle.* Geneva: Éditions Minkoff, 1976.

Dufourcq, Norbert, ed. *La Musique à la cour de Louis XIV et de Louis XV d'après les mémoires de Sourches et Luynes 1681-1758.* Paris: Éditions A. & J. Picard, 1970.

Eppelsheim, Jurgen. *Das Orchester in dem Werken Jean-Baptiste Lullys.* Tutzing: Hans Schneider, 1961.

Flagel, Claude. "La vielle parisienne sous Louis XV: un modèle pour deux siècles." *Instrumentistes et luthiers parisiens. XVIIᵉ-XIXᵉ siècles.* Ed. Florence Gétreau. Paris: Délégation à l'Action Artistique de la Ville de Paris, 1988. 117-133.

__. "Vielles de Normandie: La 'Terrassonite'!" *Revue Modale* 5 (Fall, 1984): 37-40.

Fougerit, Alain. "Fabrication des vielles en Normandie au XVIIIᵉ siècle" *Revue Modale* 3 (Winter, 1983): 6-35.

Fromenteau, Michèle et Guy Casteuble. *Musiques en duo pour vielles à roue qui conviennent aussi aux flûtes à bec alto, violons, musettes ou autres instruments.* 2 vols. Courlay: Éditions J. M. Fuzeau, 1979, 1985.

Gustafson, Bruce and David Fuller. *A Catalogue of French Harpsichord Music 1699-1780.* Oxford: Clarendon Press, 1990.

Green, Robert A. "Eighteenth-Century French Chamber Music for the Vielle." *Early Music* 15 (Nov. 1987): 468-479.

__."Title Pages of Eighteenth-Century French Chamber Music as a Guide to Performance Practice." *The Courant* 1, no.4 (Oct. 1983): 21-28.

Hefling, Stephen E. *Rhythmic Alteration in Seventeenth- and Eighteenth-Century Music. Notes Inégales and Overdotting.* New York: Schirmer Books, 1993.

Hellerstedt, Kahren Jones. "Hurdy-gurdies from Heironymous Bosch to Rembrandt." diss., U. of Pittsburgh, 1981.

Hollinger, Roland. *Les musiques à bourdons. Vielle à roue et cornemuses.* Paris: La Flûte de Pan, 1982.

Hsu, John. *A Handbook of French Baroque Viol Technique.* New York: Broude Brothers Limited, 1981.

Jorgensen, Owen. *Tuning.* East Lansing: Michigan State University Press, 1991.

Jurgens, Madeleine, *Documents du Minutier Central concernant la musique (1600-1650).* Paris: S.E.V.P.E.N., 1967.

Lapaire, Hughes. *Vielles et cornemuses.* Moulins: Crépin-Leblond, 1901.

Lefeuvre, Pascal. "La Vielle à roue. 800 ans d'évolution (2ème partie)." *Trad Magazine* (juillet\août 1993): 8-11.

Leppert, Richard D. *Arcadia at Versailles. Noble Amateur Musicians and Their Musettes and Hurdy-Gurdies at the French Court (c.1660-1789). A Visual Study.* Amsterdam and Lisse: Swets & Zeitlinger B. V., 1978.

Lindemann, Frayda B. "Pastoral Instruments in French Baroque Music: Musette and Vielle." diss. Columbia University, 1978.

Muskett, Doreen. *Method for the Hurdy-Gurdy.* 2nd ed. Piper's Croft, Bovington: Doreen and Michael Muskett, 1982.

Page, Christopher. "The Medieval *organistrum*: A Legacy from the East?" *The Galpin Society Journal* 35 (1982): 37-44.

___. "The Medieval *organistrum* and *symphonia*: 2 Terminology" *The Galpin Society Journal* 36 (1983): 71-87.

Palmer, Susann (with Samuel Palmer). *The Hurdy-Gurdy.* London &

North Pomfret: David & Charles, 1980.

Peterman, Lewis Emmanuel Jr. ""The Instrumental Chamber Music of Joseph Bodin de Boismortier With Special Emphasis on the Trio Sonatas for Two Treble Instruments and Basso Continuo." diss. University of Cincinnati College-Conservatory of Music, 1985.

Ralyea, John. *A Modest Manual for the Hurdy-Gurdy* including Charles Bâton's *Mémoire sur la Vielle en D-la-ré* as translated and annotated by Paul Goldstein. Chicago: The author, 1981.

__. *Shepherd's Delight.* Guide to the Repertoire for: Hurdy-gurdy, Musette, Organized Hurdy-gurdy, Strohfiddel, Nyckelharpa, Trumpet Marine. 2nd ed. Chicago: The author, 1981.

NOTE: also includes "The Hurdy-gurdy on the French Opera Stage: Savoyards, More Savoyards and Fanchon." and Standley Howell, "The Medieval Hurdy-gurdy."

Rault, Christian. *L'Organistrum.* Paris: Aux Amateurs de Livres, 1985.

Sadie, Stanley, ed. *The New Grove Dictionary of Music and Musiciens.* London: MacMillan Publishers Limited, 1980.

Baines, Francis, Edmund Bowles. "Hurdy-gurdy."
Bowers, Jane M. "Chédeville."
Fay, Laurel. "Joseph Bodin de Boismortier."
Fuller, David. "Michelle Corrette."
__. "Jean-Baptiste Dupuits."
Zaslaw, Neal. "Charles Bâton."

Schneider, Herbert. *Chronologisch-Thematisches Verzeichnis sämtliche Werke von Jean-Baptiste Lully.* Mainzer Studien zur Musikwissenschaft 14. Tutzing: Hans Schneider, 1981.

Straeten, Edmond van der. *La musique aux Pays-Bas,* 8 vols. Brussels: G.-A. Trigt, 1878, Dover Rep., 1969.

Tailhades, Claude. "Viellistes de Ville - Viellistes de Cour." Unpublished Essay, 1993.

Robert A. Green is Professor of Music at Northern Illinois University and author of many articles on eighteenth-century French music and performance practice. He plays the hurdy-gurdy in solo recitals and with various ensembles, and he is featured on a recording of eighteenth-century chamber music.